Lost Legends of the West

Lost Legends of the West

Brad Williams
&
Choral Pepper

First Promontory Press edition published in 1996.

Promontory Press
A division of Budget Book Service, Inc.
386 Park Avenue South
New York, NY 10016

Promontory Press is a registered trademark of Budget Book Service, Inc.

Published by arrangement with Henry Holt and Company, Inc.

Library of Congress Catalog Card Number: 70-80368

ISBN: 0-88394-093-0

Printed in the United States of America.

To Isabel

CONTENTS

Preface   ix
A Few Lost Bones   1
Pancho Villa's Lost Head   7
The Lost Remains of Mr. Quejo   19
The Lost Lover of Pearl Hart   29
The Lost Payroll at Wickenburg   36
California's Lost Diamonds   51
Henry Crabb—A Born Loser   59
A Lost Chord in Tijuana Brass   70
A Couple of Lost Squadrons   87
The Lost Woman of San Nicolas   93
Lost Arts   100
A Few Lost Ladies   108
A Couple of Lost Towns   117
A Meteoric Loss   126
The Lost Treasure of Cucamonga   132
The Lost Saints   137
The Lost Secrets of Charles Hatfield   147
Lost in Lava   157
A Trio of Lost Monsters   165
A Lost Ship of the Desert   177
Epilogue: The Lost Gold Bars of Juan Blanco   185

Sixteen pages of black and white photographs follow page 114.

PREFACE

Located some one hundred and twenty miles west of San Diego, California, is a small island nation that does not exist, a country that the United States Government would dearly like to see become lost. It has been given three names, Albonia, Aqualandia, and Taluga, and none of them appear on any map. Although its three potential rulers are squabbling among themselves, they agree that this new nation will be independent, that all of its permanent residents will be employed by the government, and that it will not be a democratic society.

The site of this country, that is not, is the Cortes Bank, a shallow reef about 12 miles wide and 35 miles long which presently is between 14 and 30 feet below the surface of the sea. The news of this emerging nation first came to public attention when motion-picture actor Joe Kirkwood, Jr., and two associates bought an old concrete-hulled freighter named *Jalisco*, announced that they were going to sink it on the reef, and that the wreck would be the cornerstone of a new land known as Albonia. The announcement was greeted with the skepticism accorded many Hollywood press releases, until Kirkwood entered a low bid with the city of Los Angeles to haul away its trash for $1.25 a ton. He told reporters that Albonia would rise on six thousand tons of solid trash a day from Los Angeles. About the same time, a Coast Guard patrol plane noticed the *Jalisco* anchored off the southwest corner of the reef.

The military took a dim view of the new nation so close to the borders of the United States and, although Albonia was some thirty miles farther from California than Cuba is from Florida, the military were successful in obtaining an injunction from the federal courts which prohibited Kirkwood from scuttling the *Jalisco*. The City of San Diego suddenly became fearful that the nation of Albonia quite possibly could break up in a heavy storm and that the city would become inundated by Los Angeles trash.

A few hours after the injunction was granted, a large swell rolled in from the Pacific, effortlessly scuttled the *Jalisco* on the spot and so, according to Kirkwood, established the cornerstone for this new nation.

It was at this point that the conflict between Albonia and the United States reached the attention of a Seattle attorney named Jack England. He promptly announced that he had claimed the reef as early as 1959, that his backers were prepared to build a new nation on the site and upon a much more solid foundation than Los Angeles rubbish. The name of the new nation was Taluga, not Albonia. He exhibited documents and artists' conceptions of the new nation with its three cities, Aurora, Bonaventura, and Tirana, and detailed plans as to how the reef would be encircled by huge granite boulders such as those used on the ten-mile levee surrounding Los Angeles Harbor. The interior then would be filled by dredging and more boulders brought out from California. Then would come the hotels, the airport, and possibly a few gambling casinos to attract the nomadic, playful American tourist.

"Kirkwood and England are both out of line," then announced Mike Austin of Los Angeles. "I claimed this nation many years ago and named it Aqualandia." He, too, produced documents and the great seal of the nation of Aqualandia which proclaimed him as regent.

The United States then began seriously to concern itself with the nation that was yet to be. United States attorney Edwin Miller of the Federal Department of Justice called a press conference in San Diego. There will be no foreign country emerging this close to the United States, he announced. Although the Cortes Bank is more than one hundred miles offshore, he said, it is located on the United States continental shelf and under the 1899 Rivers and Harbors Act, it is under United States control. "All navigable waters surrounding the United States and extending as far as the continental shelf are under our government's control," he told the Associated Press. "It is unlawful to build any construction without permission of the Army."

"The Army?"

"Yes. This is under control of the Army Corps of Engineers and the Department of the Interior," Miller replied.

This should have ended the story, but, unhappily, someone in the American Tuna Fleet Association read Miller's remarks. The Association is very sensitive to any claims of jurisdiction outside the three-mile limit of any nation. Tuna clippers more than one hundred and fifty miles at sea have been impounded by Ecuador and Peru. To have a United States attorney even hint that this country would recognize any jurisdictional claim beyond three miles was equivalent to treason. Telegrams of protest were dispatched to the President and the Congress.

Someone turned to Army Brigadier General John Dillard for comment. "We ought to blow it up," he replied. "Blow it up and the whole issue will become lost."

It was not necessary to blow up the Cortes Bank. There were no more diplomatic exchanges between the heads of government of Albonia, Aqualandia, or Taluga. In the late spring of 1969, someone telephoned Marvin Gray, a talk-show commentator in Los Angeles, and asked him if he ever had heard of the legend of the lost continent of Taluga which sank off the coast of California about a thousand years ago. Gray replied that so far as he was concerned, even the legend had become lost.

Most legends have their roots in fact, although few are so far apart as the lost continent of Taluga and an idea from a Seattle attorney. Most legends of the West evolve around something lost, ranging from mines to heads. Some of the most intriguing of these have been chosen as the theme for this book. The writers have purposely avoided the lost-mine syndrome, where derelict prospectors expire in the arms of a friendly family physician only seconds before the location of a fabulously rich gold mine can be divulged.

Such stories are not so much legend as adult fairy tales. Instead, the writers have taken legends which are known to have been based on fact and, in many instances, they have substantiated them by comparatively recent developments.

The adamant young lady who called Marvin Gray was convinced that there was a lost nation of Taluga. When the conversation was over, she was still convinced that there had been a lost nation of Taluga and that Marvin Gray was not very bright.

Legends start from fact. They are kept alive through faith.

The writers particularly wish to thank the following for the help they have given in preparing this book: The Hon. John McManus, Fred A. Carleson, John J. (Cactus Jack) Jeffrey, Dana Burden, Dora Heap, Arda Haenszel, Betty Lou Waters, Don Turner, Mick Jirack, Midge Walker, Larry Meyer, Chuck Hillinger, Jack Pepper, and Bill Knyvett.

Los Angeles, California
June 1969   *Brad Williams*
                                                   Choral Pepper

Lost Legends of the West

A FEW LOST BONES

Which my name is Bowers, and
my crust was busted
Falling down a shaft in Calavaras
County
But I'd take it kindly if you'd
send the pieces
Home to old Missouri!

—"To the Pliocene Skull,"
Bret Harte

The West certainly is the newest part of the United States, but it is equally certain that it is the oldest part of the continent. Man was living in southern California for many thousands of years before there even was a Plymouth Rock.

Probably the best authority on California's anthropological popularity is Dr. Louis S. B. Leakey, the prominent British anthropologist and archaeologist, who has come up with evidence that man was living around what is now the Mojave Desert at least 40,000 years ago, and possibly as long as 100,000 years before this section of the United States was besieged by smog. Dr. Leakey based his assumptions upon a find in the Calico Mountains

1

where 170 man-made implements were found by an archaeological team headed by Dr. Ruth D. Simpson of San Bernardino.

Finds of early human habitation are being made with remarkable regularity throughout the West, and it appears almost axiomatic that when someone digs up an ancient skull, someone other than the original owner is due for a headache.

In the Calico Mountain discovery, the headache came first to Glen S. Gunn, a prospector who held several mining claims in the area, including one that stretched across the archaeologists' trenches. At about the same time the ancient tools were discovered, Gunn discovered that the area contained valuable mineral deposits. To Gunn, the minerals were worth a lot more than a stone tool abandoned by some squatter 100,000 years ago. He promptly served an eviction notice upon the archaeologists. They took the matter up with the Bureau of Land Management, who referred it to the United States Department of the Interior. With all this pressure, Gunn stayed his eviction notice and although the issue has been solved temporarily, there is still a touch of migraine on both sides of the trenches, when either party thinks of the unreasonableness of the other.

Recently a 13,000-year-old skull was dug up near the confluence of the Snake and Palouse rivers in southeastern Washington by Professor Ronald Fryxell. The area in which this skull was found soon will be flooded by back-up waters from the new Lower Monumental Dam, a fact which causes some concern to archaeologists who would like more time for exploration than is in the present timetable. Human bones, found along with this skull, indicated that this 13,000-year-old man had provided a meal for some other 13,000-year-old neighbors. At last reports, this skull was in the possession of Senator Warren Magnuson of Washington.

About thirty-five years ago, another skull was found on what is now the outskirts of Laguna Beach, California. The skull

2

was found by Howard Wilson, who was digging in the area for arrowheads and came across it about five feet below the surface of the ground. Wilson kept his find in a shoebox for a couple of years before he reported it to the Southwest Museum in Los Angeles. Here the skull was named the Laguna Man and was described as prehistoric.

Two years later, the Laguna Man was taken to the Museum of Natural History in Santa Barbara, where an opinion was rendered that it probably belonged to a member of the "Oak Grove people" who preceded the modern California Indian. Its age was estimated at about 9,000 years. A short time later an anthropologist at the University of Southern California decided that it was once part of the skeleton of a California Indian of comparatively recent origin. The skull was returned to Wilson, who put it back in his shoebox, where it remained until 1953. In that year, he lent it to a friend who took it to experts in London, Paris, Madrid, Rome, and Brussels. The opinions of these experts were not announced publicly, but eight years elapsed before the skull of Laguna Man was returned to its shoebox in Laguna Beach.

In 1967, the discovery of the Laguna Man came to the attention of the ubiquitous Dr. Leakey. He went to Laguna, studied it, then took it to the University of California at Los Angeles. Officials at UCLA became excited and sent it on to the Smithsonian Institution in Washington where Carbon-14 tests revealed that the skull of the Laguna Man was approximately 17,000 years old. The skull of the Laguna Man started back to the shoebox, via the anthropological department at UCLA where, this time, it came to the attention of Dr. Ranier Berger. Dr. Berger made still another significant discovery. The skull of the Laguna Man was no man at all. It was the skull of a woman.

No bones have caused such furor as that raised across the nation in 1866, however, when a miner by the name of Mattison,

3

from Angels Camp, California, found a skull almost 130 feet underground in a shaft of his mine in Calavaras County. The discovery shook the foundations of Genesis. What intrigued Mr. Mattison was why some Indian would dig a grave that deep in the ground when anything over six feet would suffice. He knew the skull belonged to a very old Indian because it was fossilized and encrusted with the same kind of gravel distinctive to the earth in which he had come across it. He took it into one of the bars in Angels Camp on his next visit to town. Here he eventually ran across a doctor who told Mattison that if it was an Indian, it was a deformed one. The doctor pointed out the heavy brow ridges which extended entirely across the eyes and nose, and he pointed out several other differences in the cranium between this and other Indian skulls of a more contemporary period which were dug up occasionally around the mining camp.

The unknown doctor prevailed upon Mattison to report the find to Mr. J. D. Whitney, who, at the time, was the geologist for the State of California. Although Whitney knew nothing about skulls, he was an excellent geologist and when he was shown the gravel-encrusted skull, he checked it with the gravel in its burial place and found the two to match. The skull had been found under four strata of lava and three strata of gold-bearing gravels and thus, Whitney reported, it probably had been buried near the end of the Pliocene Era, or roughly a million years earlier.

If the announcement had been restricted to the area around Angels Camp, everyone probably would have laughed and the skull probably would have wound up as back-bar furniture in some tavern. Whitney announced the discovery, however, in San Francisco, thus incurring the immediate enmity of most of the nation's clergy who knew that Adam was the first man that ever was invented and he wasn't anywhere near a million years old.

Whitney discovered that he had some other enemies also.

4

Some months earlier, because of his testimony, some local San Francisco financiers had become considerably embarrassed when caught selling stock in mining properties which were worthless and had been forced to refund investors large sums of money. This group immediately sided with the clergy, accusing Whitney of heresy and questioning Whitney's mental health, as well as his qualifications as a geologist. One of these confidence men called in the press and announced that the skull really was the property of an Angels Camp dentist and had been planted in the mine as a practical joke on Mattison. He even displayed a headless skeleton, which he said had been in the fictional Dr. Kelley's office.

Anthropologists joined in the attack upon Whitney because, if the skull was a million years old, it destroyed every theory on record about the age of man on earth. Whitney apparently had a remarkable disposition. He kept the skull and whenever he was questioned about it, he would reply that the skull had been discovered *in situ* (that it had not been planted where it was found), and that the area in which it had been found dated back to the end of the Pliocene Era. He did not get upset even over such vitriolic attacks as one from a high-spirited evangelist who claimed that God had told him that Whitney was in reality Satan and that there was no such thing as the Pliocene Era.

The charges were raised constantly for almost fifteen years, until finally Whitney, with Mattison's permission, sent the notorious skull to the Peabody Museum of Archaeology and Ethnology in Cambridge, Massachusetts.

In 1903, Professor John C. Merriam of the Museum solved the controversy with diplomatic finesse. In a paper read before the Anthropological Association, Merriam said, "Taken as a whole, the problem seemed to present as remarkable a case of absolutely contradictory evidence as ever has appeared in science or law. After so long a lapse of years, it will probably never be possible to trace out the history of the Calavaras Skull with certainty." He added that Whitney was right in stating that the skull came from a very ancient cave deposit, "but how ancient is still a matter to be determined."

The skull is still in the Peabody Museum at Harvard. Its age will never be known. "From the condition of its finding it will never be possible to get any kind of a date for it," W. W. Howells, Professor of Anthropology at Harvard, recently told the writers.

In Angels Camp, they have a different memory of the skull. "Isn't anything to it," one old-timer said recently. "Now, if I remember correctly, someone took the skull from a dentist's office and planted it in a mineshaft as a joke. The dentist just got so mad about it, he just up and left town."

Bret Harte apparently was not convinced as to its authenticity either. Its discovery prompted his writing an ode "To the Pliocene Skull."

There is still another skull that figures prominently in the lore of the West, but unlike the Calavaras skull, this one has yet to be found.

PANCHO VILLA'S LOST HEAD

Fly, fly, little dove
Perch among the castor beans
And tell to all the gringos
That Pancho Villa's dead.
—Mexican Mariachi Song

Early in the morning of July 20, 1923, Francisco "Pancho" Villa was assassinated in the small city of Parral, Mexico, a few miles south of Chihuahua. Two and one half years later, his grave at Parral was broken open and Villa's head was severed from his body. There have been many theories advanced as to the reason for this. The most popular in Mexico is that the United States wanted proof that Villa was really dead and offered a $50,000 reward to the first person who could deliver Villa's head in El Paso. Most scholars scoff at this solution to the riddle, yet recently there died in New Mexico an old man who may have found the answer to this mystery. It is not far removed from the popular thought in Mexico. The key to the posthumous decapitation is the notorious raid by Villa on the sleepy New Mexican town of Columbus in the early morning hours of March 9, 1916.

In 1915, President Woodrow Wilson recognized Venustiano Carranza as the head of government for Mexico, a diplomatic gesture which upset several of the revolutionary contenders for the oft-changing presidency. Of all the applicants, Villa was the most vehement in expressing his disapproval. The first positive indication of his anger came on January 10, 1916, when a section of his army, commanded by Rafael Castro and Pablo Lopez, ambushed a train near Santa Isabel in Chihuahua. On the train was a large party of North American mining engineers and miners. All had been assured of safe passage by a recently installed Carrancista governor in Chihuahua who needed the mining experts to help reopen a long-closed mine.

Villa stopped the train, robbed all of the passengers, then shot and killed sixteen of the North American mining experts to demonstrate that Carranza was not in a position to guarantee safe passage to anyone in northern Mexico.

The second demonstration of his rage came two months later when a horde of Villistas swept across the border and attacked Columbus, thus assuring the loss of Pancho's head a little less than a decade later. Villa quite probably was motivated by reasons other than revenge for his assault on Columbus. The Thirteenth Cavalry Encampment was stationed here and they were well supplied with arms, ammunition, and other vital military equipment which Villa needed desperately. Villa also had some unfinished business with one of his major suppliers, Sam Ravel, who operated a general store in the town. When President Wilson recognized the Carranza government, the United States embargoed all arms shipments to Villa. Ravel had been one of Villa's principal suppliers and had accepted payment for another shipment immediately prior to the embargo. Having already purchased the arms he could not deliver, Ravel thought it poor business to refund the money to Villa until he had found another customer.

At the time of the raid, the warden of the New Mexico State Penitentiary was a young man named John B. McManus. A native of Ireland, McManus had lived in Wisconsin briefly, then headed for the West, where he got a job as a telegrapher for the railroad in Columbus. In 1912, shortly after New Mexico was admitted to the Union, McManus was appointed warden by Governor W. C. McDonald, whom he had met when McDonald was in Columbus.

McManus had a great fondness for Mexico, particularly the wide desert country in the northern part of that nation. He spoke a "bastard Spanish, enough to get by on." Early in March of 1916, he had gone to visit friends in El Paso, Texas. In spite of warnings that Villa was on a rampage, he crossed the border into Juárez, where he bought a horse. He then started out on a cross-country trip just below the border, planning to re-enter the United States near Columbus, where he would stay with friends a few days before returning to Santa Fe.

On the morning of the raid, McManus was sleeping on the desert a few miles south of Columbus. He was awakened abruptly by the thrust of a rifle muzzle in his belly and was surrounded by what appeared to be an army. As he struggled out of his blanket, he heard one of the Mexicans order that he be shot. Another instantly countermanded the order, warning that the shot might be heard by someone else ahead of them who would alert the town.

There was a brief discussion. "Who would be sleeping on the desert?"

"Here is one," a bandit said. "If there is one, there may be some others."

The argument seemed reasonable. McManus was led to his

horse, lifted onto its back, and then his feet were tied together by a rope passing beneath the animal's belly. His saddle, his blankets, and other gear disappeared somewhere amid the mass of silent men. A bandanna was placed in his mouth as a gag and a line was attached to the horse's bridle, with the other end fastened to the saddle of one of the bandits.

The thought that remained with McManus for the rest of his life was a wonder as to how so many men could move so silently and so swiftly. Not a man uttered a word. Even the horses seemed to be trained to be quiet, as the bandit army moved across the desert toward Columbus. When they arrived at the small town, three of the bandits went ahead. A moment later, by the light of the moon, McManus saw one of them climb a pole and cut the telegraph wires. The falling of the wires was a signal, for suddenly the bandits swooped down upon the town and its adjacent military encampment, screaming and shouting and shooting their rifles.

McManus' horse was cut loose from the other, but it raced along with the bandits into the center of the town.

For more than two hours, McManus watched the looting of stores and of the military base from his uncomfortable bare-backed-perch on the high-withered horse. The animal, untethered and not in the least disconcerted by the gunfire, ambled around the town, pausing occasionally to nibble a tuft of grass.

Villa himself did not accompany his horde on the raid, but everyone in Columbus thought he did because of the raiders' constant cries of "Viva Villa, Viva Mexico!" Soon they were answered by cries in Spanish of, "One thousand dollars for Villa's head!"

Sam Ravel's store was first to be looted and put to the torch, then went the others, but there was no organized resistance, except mistakenly when one gang of bandits raced around the corner of a building and was cut down by gunfire from another gang. Through it all, McManus and the horse wandered about

10

unscathed. Bodies were lying everywhere on the streets and the screams of the dying mingled eerily with the cries of the bandits still praising their leader. McManus was convinced that his luck could not last.

The raid ended with the arrival of the false dawn. As the bandits began their retreat, one galloped up to McManus and raised his rifle. Then he paused and stared at McManus with an expressionless face. Suddenly he laughed and placed the rifle back into a saddle holster. He next quickly picked up the line to the bridle and, with McManus still tied to the animal, galloped after his companions with the horse in tow. The ride was incredibly painful. McManus' feet were tied under the animal's belly, but his hands had been left free so he was able to hold his balance on the horse's back by wrapping his arms around its neck.

About two hours later, when well inside of Mexico, the bandits paused. The man who had been towing McManus and the horse dismounted and walked a short distance ahead to confer with some men who apparently also held positions of rank in the Villa forces. By now, McManus was in such pain that he was in a semiconscious condition. Only vaguely was he aware of being the subject of conversation among the bandit leaders. Occasionally they stared at him and gesticulated. Finally, all but one shrugged and turned away.

The exception walked back toward him. It was the same man who had hesitated before taking him captive in Columbus. The bandit untied the ropes that bound McManus' feet under the horse and then, as McManus started to fall, the bandit helped him to the ground. McManus could not stand upright. The circulation in his legs had been cut off too long. When he sank to the sand, expecting to be executed, the bandit laughed. Slowly, he began to massage McManus' legs.

"I do you a favor," he said presently, in Spanish. "You understand?"

McManus nodded.

11

"Then someday maybe you will do me a favor?"

Again McManus nodded. He wanted to be a hero but he was too frightened.

The bandit laughed again, rose, and led the horse over to some others that had been captured from the United States Cavalry Encampment. Presently he returned, carrying a United States Army canteen full of water and a piece of dried beef. These he gave to McManus. Ten minutes later, the Villa horde was gone. An hour later, McManus was able to move and start his painful journey back to Columbus. Afterward, he could never understand how he was able to make his way on foot back to the border, but shortly before dark he was intercepted by a military patrol on the North American side and was given a horse. He rode "sidesaddle" the rest of the way into Columbus. The first night he spent in military custody. Interrogators found it difficult to believe his story, but eventually they released him.

The raid had been a costly one for Villa. Approximately five hundred men had crossed the border and of these, exactly one hundred had been killed in Columbus. The raiders, however, had taken back with them more than one hundred of the cavalry's horses and most of its arsenal, including machine guns and rifles. Eighteen Americans had been killed, eight wounded, and virtually everyone in the town had been robbed of money and any possessions of value to the raiders. Sam Ravel lost his shipment of arms which had been destined for the Villa forces.

There were many repercussions from the raid. The United States, over the objections of the Carranza government it so recently had recognized, sent in troops on a punitive expedition commanded by General John Pershing. The expedition never could find Villa nor any of his men, but three months after the raid, Pershing found himself fighting Carranza forces who objected to the invasion. In June there was a battle near Carrizal, in which General Felix U. Gomez, along with eighty-four men, was killed. Eight United States soldiers also lost their lives in this engagement.

Peace talks were scheduled and held in New London, Connecticut, and Atlantic City, New Jersey, but they amounted to nothing. Pershing continued his futile search for Villa in Chihuahua, while at the same time, Villa issued manifestos accusing Carranza of allowing Mexico to be invaded by filibusterers. On two separate occasions, Villa captured Chihuahua City, the capital of Chihuahua, but by the time Pershing's troops arrived, Villa once again had melted into the vast desert of northern Mexico. Pershing kept up his chase for a year and a half, at a cost of some 130 million dollars, before he and his troops finally were recalled for bigger and better wars in Europe.

The Villa forces continued their raids and occasional kidnappings of United States citizens for ransom until after the assassination of Carranza and the assumption of power by Provisional President de la Huerta. It was under Huerta that Villa agreed to go into retirement. As part of the package, he was given a large hacienda at Parral where, on July 20, 1923, he was assassinated, presumably at the order of Huerta's successor, Plutarco Elias Calles.

McManus continued as warden of the New Mexico State Penitentiary in Santa Fe, active in the state's Democratic party and in civic affairs in the state capital. In 1925, McManus was interviewed in Albuquerque by a reporter who was writing a story on the Columbus raid. When McManus related in detail his harrowing experience on that night he mentioned that he still could not understand why his life had been spared.

About a week after the story appeared in the Albuquerque newspaper, McManus received a call in his office from a Mexican who, in broken English, said he would like to talk with him about the Pancho Villa raid on Columbus. At first, McManus demurred, replying politely in Spanish that his schedule was rather heavy.

13

"There was one time a man spared your life and you promised him a favor in return," the caller said.

They met in the bar at La Fonda Hotel about two hours later. The man was in his late fifties. He was wearing a suit with a high starched collar and, from the manner in which he wore it, McManus knew that he was unused to it. His name, the man said, was Marino Contreras and he was the brother of Ramon Contreras.

McManus nodded politely. There was nothing familiar about the man or the name.

"It was my brother, Ramón, who took you on the horse from Columbus and twice spared your life," Contreras said casually.

"I have never been on a horse since that time," McManus replied. He decided that as a result of the story, the man was going to "borrow" some money. "I am grateful to your brother," he said aloud. "This must be apparent."

"My brother now is dead."

"I am sorry to hear that." McManus glanced at his watch. "What is it that you want?"

Marino Contreras told the following story. His brother had not been motivated by any feeling of compassion when he spared McManus' life. It was a matter of war and McManus was of the enemy. Ramón, however, had realized that the raid on Columbus quite possibly was a mistake and that quite probably Villa would meet the fate of all other revolutionaries in the long struggle for power in Mexico. When this happened, it would be a profitable venture to collect the thousand-dollar reward that had been offered in Columbus for the head of Pancho Villa. The favor that would be asked of McManus, in return for his life, was that he act as intermediary in collecting this money.

During the ensuing weeks, the plan of Ramón Contreras had been forgotten and then, two-and-one-half years after Villa's assassination, it had been recalled. It was Ramón, Marino said,

14

who had broken into Villa's grave and severed the head from the cadaver. Ramón then had taken the head to Columbus, had buried it there in a well-protected box, and had gone looking for Mc-Manus. While he was asking questions in the Columbus station, he had been arrested by the United States border patrol and escorted back across the border.

"He said the town had rebuilt itself very well," Marino said.

McManus smiled. "You want one thousand dollars?" he asked.

Marino shook his head. "I know the location of Villa's head," he replied. "I will take you there and then we will divide the reward, half for you and half for me."

Again McManus smiled. He had not known that Villa's corpse had been decapitated. At the same time, he marveled at the rashness of the man, approaching a state officer with his confidence game. "Do you have papers to be in the United States?" he asked.

Marino gave him a disappointed look. "My brother spared your life," he said.

"Then it is to your brother that I owe the favor."

Marino Contreras said nothing, stood up, and walked out of the hotel. McManus debated whether or not to report the illegal entry to the police, then decided it was not worth the effort. The man probably would be picked up anyway within the next few days.

Some weeks later, at a political gathering, McManus related his experience to Dennis Chavez, who later was to become a United States senator from New Mexico. Chavez chuckled and replied that a reward of one thousand dollars for Villa's head was a rather small amount at that time. "The government spent one hundred thirty million dollars trying to catch Villa," he commented.

It was at this moment that McManus realized that there

15

had been no reward posted in Columbus. The thousand-dollar figure had only been cried out by the Columbus citizens and the United States soldiers in reply to the bandits' cries of "Viva Villa." The mental picture of his experience swiftly flashed through his head. Only someone who was there could have known of it. Contreras could have been one of the bandits. Or he could have been telling the truth.

John McManus had a friend who was a professor at the University of New Mexico in Albuquerque, a man who was Mexican and an authority on Mexican history. The next time McManus was in Albuquerque, he called upon his friend and turned the subject of the conversation to Villa. The professor became fascinated by the story and, after dinner, the two men spent the evening going through the professor's private library, which dealt primarily with Mexican history.

It had been shortly after seven in the morning when Pancho Villa left the home of his mistress in the Calle Zaragoza in Parral to return to his hacienda in Canutillo. He was driving a Dodge touring car which, in addition to himself, contained five members of his bodyguard and a servant. The bodyguard consisted of Rosalío Rosales, Daniel Tamayo, Rafael Medrano, Claro Hurtado, and a man named Ramón Contreras.

Approximately two blocks distant, at the intersection of the Calle Juarez and the Calle Gabino Barreda, an eight-man band of assassins, led by Melitón Lozoya, were hiding in a two-room house. Each was armed with an automatic pistol and an automatic rifle. Villa would have to turn into the intersection and cross a plaza to get to Canutillo. The lookout for the assassins was a street peddler who mopped his face with a bandanna as Villa approached.

The assassins first fired a fusillade from the windows of the house and then, as the Dodge careened into a tree, they raced out of the building firing pistols. Villa was able to kill one of his

16

attackers before he died. Only one man in the Villa party escaped: Ramón Contreras. Although wounded, he managed to roll into the bottom of a dry riverbed and work his way back to the home of Villa's mistress, where a doctor was summoned to sew up his wounds. That night, he left on horseback for Canutillo.

A few days later, McManus wrote to the *jefe politico* in Chihuahua asking if a picture were available of Ramón Contreras. He wrote also to the widow of Pancho Villa to ask what had happened to Ramón Contreras after his arrival at Canutillo, the day after the assassination.

The *jefe politico* was able to secure a picture of Ramón Contreras. It looked like the same man, but McManus never was sure. The *jefe politico* wrote also that no one apparently knew what had happened to Ramón, but he was believed to be operating a business with his brother Marino in Juarez. The widow of the former bandit did not answer McManus' letter.

McManus asked the police in Juarez to locate Marino Contreras, but they were unable to do so. About ten years later, McManus ran across an old picture of Villa and his wife with an "unidentified" man standing in the background. It was a better picture than that sent by the *jefe politico* of Chihuahua. There was no doubt in McManus' mind but that the picture was that of the man who had pulled him on a horse into Mexico after the Columbus raid.

Once again, McManus started his search for Marino, but he was as unsuccessful as before. The man had vanished as completely as had Ramón.

Today, ironically, the sleepy town of Columbus, New Mexico, has become a monument to Villa's raid. There is a state park which bears his name, most bars display his picture, and many stores sell "genuine souvenirs" of the audacious assault. The widow of the famous bandit has been named an honorary citizen of the community.

17

There is a strong possibility that the most genuine souvenir of all, the head of Pancho Villa, lies in a well-protected box somewhere within the town limits.

There is no mystery at all, however, as to what happened to the remains of another Western renegade. There are three skulls and heads and skeletons, all belonging to the same man.

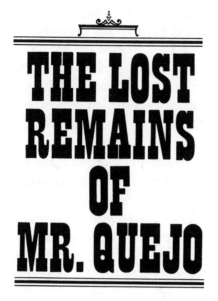

THE LOST REMAINS OF MR. QUEJO

Mr. Quejo's first name, if he ever had one, has been lost in history. Half-Indian and half-white, he hated whites and Indians equally and with reasonable justification. His mother was a beautiful Indian lass of the Cocopah tribe and his father was presumed to be a passing prospector who raped her shortly after the turn of the century.

The Cocopahs shared a belief with most Indians in the Southwest that anyone with white blood was bad, even if it was only half white, so shortly after Quejo was born, the tribal priest performed a religious ceremony which absolved the young lass. He then proceeded to throw the infant over the side of a nearby cliff, thus presuming that he had adequately solved a local problem of miscegenation.

That evening, while the village slept, the young mother crept out to the base of the cliff and found to her amazement and joy that the child still lived. She picked him up and fled with him in her arms up the shores of the Colorado River until the steep channel forced her inland to the caves of Pyramid Canyon.

There was no solution to her dilemma. No Cocopah village would accept her with her halfbreed son. She was too far distant from any white settlement to seek aid, and it is unlikely that such a thought occurred to her any more than the idea that she might receive aid from another tribe. She never was able to solve her problem.

Several weeks later, two Paiute Indians found her dead on the desert floor beside a broken barrel-cactus from which she had tried to squeeze water. Still alive and sucking on the dead woman's breast was the infant Quejo. The Paiutes buried the young mother and brought the child back to their camp, where there was no taboo against miscegenation. It was a humanitarian gesture that in the ensuing years was to cost at least twenty-three persons their lives.

Quejo grew up in the Paiute camp, sometimes doing odd jobs for the whites in mining communities along the Colorado River. In some ways he showed a remarkable talent for learning. By the time he was in his early teens, he was an expert horseman, a marksman, and a superb tracker. His English was intelligible and the miners he worked for always remarked that the "halfbreed" was more energetic than most of the local Paiutes. Never, however, did he participate in Indian games with other Paiutes his age, and at night he would withdraw from the others and sit alone. Paiute youths who knew of his background taunted him constantly, usually with insults referring to his being half a white man.

20

One night, soon after he had turned twenty, he sat alone, as usual, when a Paiute youth with the unlikely name of Bismarck casually referred to him once again as a white man. Quejo slowly rose and went over to the corral where he blanketed and haltered one of the horses. No one paid any attention. Quejo often rode off by himself in the night. This night, however, was different. After he had mounted the horse, Quejo walked the animal close to the fire, raised his rifle and shot Bismarck in the back of the head. Then he raced away.

The startled Paiutes set off in pursuit moments later, but they were unable to find any trace of Quejo. It was to set a pattern. In subsequent years, neither Indian nor white posses ever were able to follow Quejo after one of his murders. He simply melted into the night. No one ever found out where he slept, yet, so far as anyone knew, he was never more than one hundred miles from the Paiute camp where he was raised.

His next two victims were also Paiutes with whom he had grown up. He shot one in the back and the other in the stomach, stealing into their camp at dawn while they were watering the horses. The latter victim was able to identify his assailant before he died. The remaining members of the camp, a poor and desultory band of the once-great Paiutes, swore revenge but when they were unable to pick up his trail after a short chase, they decided that he was hiding out among the whites and they soon forgot their oaths.

Quejo was not to become ignored by the whites, however. An elderly man named Woodward was found by his wife near a woodpile outside of a small homestead in southern Nevada. He had been shot in the back of the head after his assailant had forced him to remove all of his clothes. Before he died, Woodward was able to identify the murderer as Quejo, whom he had once hired to help him clear some land.

While a posse was being formed, word arrived that the

21

operator of the Gold Bug Mill, about five miles distant on the Colorado River, also had been shot and his body stripped of clothing. The posse scouted the area for two weeks before giving up the hunt. Warrants were issued for Quejo's arrest and reward notices were posted that he was wanted dead or alive, but no one could find Quejo.

The most diabolical thing about Quejo's method was the long interval that passed between his murders. He waited until he was almost forgotten, then struck at some isolated farm and with his 30-30 rifle shot another victim in the head. Usually they lived just long enough to identify him. When they didn't, it was Quejo's method of murder and a total lack of motive that pointed the posse in his direction.

On one paradoxical occasion, however, two brothers were riding into Searchlight, Nevada, after an unsuccessful prospecting trip. It was near dusk when they noticed a man on a horse following them at some distance. When the brothers trotted their horses, so did the man behind them trot his. When they walked their horses, he walked his. A few miles beyond the limits of town, the brothers decided to turn into an arroyo that skirted a craggy mountain studded with cholla and pocked with caves. Both of the brothers thought of Quejo and when they heard hoofbeats against the rocks of the arroyo and knew that the stranger was determinedly stalking them, they became certain that he was the notorious renegade.

When they reached a steep draw that ascended the bank of the arroyo, they raced their horses up it and into a crevice in the mountain which, to their consternation, proved to be a cul de sac. It was too late to expose themselves back at its entrance, so they quickly dismounted and waited, with guns drawn. Soon the shadowy outline of the mounted figure appeared at the entrance to the cul de sac. One of the brothers raised his revolver.

"Suppose he is not Quejo," the other one whispered.

22

One of the brothers called out, "Quejo!"

Still the horseman did not answer, but he backed his mount slowly away until his outline had dropped below the bank. Neither brother could hear a sound after he disappeared.

An hour later both men still were pondering their dilemma. There was no way to tell if the mysterious horseman outside was Quejo. On the other hand, there was no way to tell if he was not Quejo. By his actions, he had proved that he was not a friend, however, and rather than taking the risk of walking into an ambush in the dark, the two men decided to spend the rest of the night in the comparative safety of the cul de sac.

When the sun rose the following morning, the brother who was taking his turn as guard noticed a flash of light on the canyon wall across from him. Then he noticed another and still another, as the sun's rays passed over the jagged outcropping. He awakened his brother and pointed out the phenomenon. The mysterious flashes lasted another few minutes, then disappeared.

A short time later, the brothers saddled their horses and cautiously rode to the entrance of the canyon. A careful search in the area disclosed no signs of the sinister stranger from the previous night. The two brothers then returned for a closer examination of the wall that had reflected the sun's rays. With a sudden surge of elation, they realized that they were rich. Through the wall of the canyon ran a vein of quartz webbed through with wires of pure gold. It was one of the richest strikes to be found in gold-laden Searchlight, Nevada.

In later years, whenever one of the brothers would hear tales of Quejo's murders, he would smile enigmatically and reply only, "Well, he has a good side, too."

In 1919, Quejo committed the unforgivable sin. He murdered a woman, a white one. Mrs. Edward Bacon, the wife of a mine supervisor at El Dorado, was heating water on a wood-burning stove preparatory to washing her dishes, when a stalking figure wearing Levis and with long black hair held in place by a red band around his forehead, entered her open kitchen door. She gave one piercing shriek as he fired his rifle into her breast. At the same time, her husband, who was working at the mine, experienced an unaccountable premonition of fear. He dashed from his office, leaped upon the saddled horse of a friend and raced to his home and discovered his dying wife.

That Quejo had murdered a white woman, a species still rare to the West, hit a new low in depravity. This launched a manhunt that was to continue for twenty-one years. During that time, Quejo murdered sixteen victims, all within a one-hundred-mile radius of Las Vegas.

On one occasion, a posse led by Clark County Deputy Sheriff Frank Wait employed a Paiute, appropriately named Tracker, who was reknown for his tracking abilities. The Indian followed Quejo's trail for four days through the malpais of the Colorado River canyon where Lake Mojave now lies, and northward up the shore of the Overton Arm of present Lake Mead. The men drove their horses unmercifully over the hot red sands of the Valley of Fire and through its steep ravines until, at last, they came upon Quejo's lair, but once again their quarry had disappeared. His hideout was a small cave and in it were the clothes of several of his victims. More ironic, there were supplies of groceries, including a can of peaches from a Las Vegas market. Tracker was unable to find any trace of Quejo's trail leading away from the hideout.

A few days later, a family of four was killed on the Arizona side of the Colorado, but all had died before the shooting was discovered, so it is not certain that this was the work of the renegade Quejo. The last murder directly attributed to him also involved a woman.

In 1930, Mrs. Edward Douglas, who lived on the outskirts of Searchlight, rode into town in the family buckboard, accompanied by her four-year-old son and husband. She dropped her husband off at the assaying office where he worked, then proceeded to the general store where she picked up a week's supply of groceries. About an hour later, she returned to her home and noticed that a horse with its reins trailing on the ground stood near the door. Her first thought was one of relief, that a man was around to help her carry the supplies into the house.

Swinging her son to the ground, she entered the kitchen, then froze in fright. A man dressed in Levis, a blue shirt, and moccasins, was on his hands and knees on the kitchen floor, uttering strange staccato sounds. Incredibly, she realized that the man was pushing her son's red toy automobile around the floor, imitating the exhaust of an automobile engine, in the manner of a child.

At first, the stranger did not appear to notice her, but soon he rose slowly to his feet. It was at this point that she suddenly remembered the warning about Quejo.

The man bent down, picked up the toy and pushed it into his waistband. When he straightened up again she saw the rifle in his hand. She screamed once, before he shot her in the neck. He then turned the rifle toward the frightened boy and hesitated. Looking at the toy car in his waistband, he lowered the rifle and slowly stepped over the screaming woman. At the door he stopped again and considered the boy, while the agonized mother continued to scream. Abruptly he turned and walked from the house.

The woman lived just long enough to tell the story to a passing miner, who had come to the house when he thought it suspicious that her boy should be wandering unattended along the road. An hour later, the posse was in full chase.

No one ever saw Quejo alive again, but it was a long time before any woman in southeastern Nevada felt safe alone in her house, and many a tough man refused to travel through uninhabited country without a companion.

On February 20, 1940, two Las Vegas residents, Arthur

Schroeder and Charles Kenyon, discovered a partially sealed cave along a precipitous trail near Willow Beach on the Arizona side of the Colorado River. Pulling aside the rocks that disguised the entrance, the two men found a clothed, mummified skeleton. In the cave were a rifle, some ammunition, rusted cans of fruit, a belt, and a string of Indian beads. Clutched in the skeletal fingers of the remains was a red toy automobile.

There was no mystery as to why the cave entrance had been blocked. It was an old Indian custom. Caves that held the dead were always sealed in order to keep coyotes and other scavengers from reaching the corpse.

Kenyon and Schroeder reported their discovery to Deputy Sheriff Frank Wait when they returned to Las Vegas. A short time later, Wait and a couple of other deputies went to the cave, picked up the mummy, and took it to an undertaker in Boulder City, a small town adjacent to Hoover Dam, a few miles south of Las Vegas.

For a few days, no one was particularly enthusiastic about either the corpse or the mystery of its grave, although Kenyon did enjoy telling of the skeleton he had found of a grown Indian holding a red toy automobile. Eventually Kenyon heard the story of Quejo and the little red car. He also heard that the Nevada State Legislature had long ago posted a reward for Quejo dead or alive in the amount of ten thousand dollars. Understandably, Kenyon and Schroeder drove out to Boulder City and asked the undertaker for the body they had found.

The undertaker sadly shook his head. He had no legal right, he explained, to release the body to anyone except a law-enforcement officer or a relative, and Kenyon failed to qualify on either count. The mortician indicated also that he had reason to believe that the mummy was that of Quejo, pointing out to Kenyon that if no one appeared to pay the mounting mortuary bills, the remains probably would have to be placed on exhibit to recoup expenses. This apparently gave Kenyon another idea, as he went to the Elks Club of Las Vegas for help.

Every year there is a Chamber of Commerce type of celebration in Las Vegas known as Helldorado, a promotion extensively supported by the Fraternal Order of Elks. Kenyon, an enthusiastic Elk, promised the Order that he would exhibit the remains in a Helldorado booth for a week before taking it to the state capital in Carson City if his Brothers would help him get the corpse away from the undertaker. At the same time, he sued the mortician.

The court ruling was handed down quickly. The only person who had a legal right to Quejo's body was the coroner unless it was proved to the satisfaction of the court that a legal heir existed.

The undertaker was unimpressed. "Either I get paid or I am going to bury it or exhibit it," he declared.

Before he could do either, the heirs began to appear. First on the scene were two Indians, one right after the other, and both claiming to be grand-nephews of Quejo. Each said the other was lying and each claimed the right to obtain the body for exhibition. Court hearings had hardly started on these cases when a third Indian arrived in Las Vegas.

It was true, he said, that both of the other Indians were grand-nephews of Quejo. He, however, was the grandson of Quejo and could testify on this authority that the corpse in possession of the mortician was not that of Quejo the murderer, although, he admitted, it might be that of some other person named Quejo.

The grandson then went on to reveal that he just happened to have the real Quejo's skeleton in his possession and that he would be perfectly willing to exhibit it, if the price was right. His story had barely made the papers when still another grandson showed up with an "authentic" Quejo skeleton.

The courts sighed collectively and pigeonholed all of the contenders' claims.

When the courts lost interest, the mortician entombed his cadaver in a casket with a sealed glass lid and exhibited it at county fairs. The owners of the other Indian mummies promptly booked theirs for display also.

All three of Quejo's disputed bodies have now become lost. The most likely exhibit, the one entombed by the mortician in a glass-lidded coffin, spent its last public days in a Las Vegas Strip museum, until the Strip became too crowded with crap tables to tolerate such things as museums. The man who owned the museum then took it out to his ranch in an area now called Paradise Valley. There, the glass-topped coffin remained propped in an abandoned bathtub in the backyard, until a new housing development overgrew the whole area and Quejo's remains disappeared as adroitly as if he had just committed another murder.

If anyone ever does find the skeleton and he can prove it is that of Quejo, he can still take it to Carson City and collect the $10,000 reward. It has never been canceled.

THE LOST LOVER OF PEARL HART

The Arizona Territorial Prison was a Devil's Island of the desert, although penologists of the late nineteenth century described it as an "ideal institution." Instead of being surrounded by impenetrable jungle, it was circled by a bleak desert. Indians were promised a standing reward of fifty dollars for every escaped prisoner they returned, much to the annoyance of many an innocent prospector who found himself bound to a mule and carted off to Yuma just in hopes that the trip might prove profitable to the Indian who affected the capture.

The Yuma prison came equipped with a dungeon, a "snake den," so named because it was a haven for resting transient rattlesnakes and scorpions. There are probably few sites more admirably suited for the location of a penitentiary. It was located on a high granite bluff that formed the junction of the Gila and the Colorado rivers, thus two sides of the jail were protected by natural moats. Across the rivers were only the rolling sands of the Colorado Desert. To the rear of the promontory was the town of Yuma.

The prison yard was surrounded by high granite walls and the cells had been blasted out of the granite block. On the north corner of the wall was a tank stand and on top of this was a sentry with a Gatling gun. Along the tops of the other three walls guards paced back and forth. The Gatling gun, a rapid-firing weapon with revolving barrels, was mounted on a two-wheeled carriage in order that it could be pointed in any direction instantly, and it probably was as strong a deterrent to escape as was the surrounding terrain.

Despite all of these hazards, there were many attempted breaks. One of the first superintendents, Thomas Gates, was taken prisoner and stabbed so severely in one of these breaks that he never fully recovered. He was followed by a Captain F. S. Ingalls, whose son was a guard and whose wife was sufficiently trained in the operation of the Gatling gun to break up at least one attempt at mass escape. Occasionally a prisoner would escape. He usually was a trustee who would take a guard as a hostage and a shield from the bullets of the Gatling gun, but these occasions were rare.

The two most remarkable departures from this grim fortress were accomplished separately by lovers, John Boot and Pearl Hart. John Boot simply vanished. One day he was there; and the next day he was not. Pearl followed him a few months later and the manner of her departure was most extraordinary. Pearl was a most extraordinary woman, as can be attested to by the fact that she was one of only three women ever imprisoned in the Yuma jail.

She was a young woman, under twenty-one, with long black hair, full breasts, and a small body, when she first entered the Arizona Territorial Prison with John Boot. She was as trustworthy as an ocelot and could swear "like a well-traveled sailor."

She and her lover had drifted into Arizona from Kansas and shortly after their arrival there began a series of stage holdups in the Territory that at first followed the same pattern. On an isolated section of a trail, a stagecoach driver suddenly would be hailed for help by a disheveled young woman obviously distraught and the victim of foul play. As soon as the stage was stopped, out stepped John Boot with a revolver in each hand. The distraught young woman then would produce her own revolver and relieve the passengers of their possessions, while Boot would take care of the express box and the mail. As soon as word of this *modus operandi* spread through the Territory, Pearl and John resorted to the more familiar pattern of holdup by just stepping out of some place of concealment as the coach approached. There was a rash of murders about the same time, but the killings were always of lone travelers. They started with the stage robberies and they ended when a posse finally caught up with Pearl and Boot and deposited them in the Pinal County Jail at Florence, Arizona.

At Florence, however, there were no accommodations for women, so Pearl was taken to the Pima County Jail in Tucson to await trial. She remained there only overnight. The next day, the turnkey discovered that Pearl had cut a hole through a thin partition and escaped. On the same night, John Boot had, in some mysterious manner, disappeared from his cell in Florence. About a week later, both John and Pearl inadvertently rode into a posse that was looking for some cattle rustlers near Deming, New Mexico.

The lovers were immediately taken back to Florence and tried on the day they arrived. Boot was sentenced to thirty years

31

in the Arizona Territorial Penitentiary, but the judge hesitated when it came to pronouncing sentence upon the eighteen-year-old Pearl.

"What in hell are you waiting for, you silly old bastard?" Pearl asked the judge mildly.

The judge quickly overcame his reluctance. "Five years in the same place," he said.

Ingalls was not happy about having a woman as a prisoner. He had to have six tier bunks ripped out of one cell and boards placed across the cell bars to ensure her the privacy needed by a female. A dressmaker in Yuma was employed to make her a special uniform.

When Pearl and John Boot arrived, however, Pearl was wearing tight jeans, a man's blouse and was smoking a cigarette, all three of which were considered most unladylike at that time. In contrast, Boot was quiet, well spoken, and he seemed to sigh with relief when he was separated from his mistress.

Mrs. Ingalls was on hand to escort Pearl to her new cell and to explain the house rules. "We'd better keep that woman far away from the other inmates," she told her husband. "She'll shock them with her language and corrupt their morals."

Ingalls kept her away from the inmates, but he could not keep Pearl quiet. She cursed constantly. One of her favorite pastimes was to call out through the bars of her cell for some man to come and join her, an invitation which so upset most of the inmates "that they would howl like coyotes all during the night." Ingalls ordered that the only person to be allowed in the cell block where Pearl was residing would be his wife with a guard, or himself.

Boot was a model prisoner. He responded to orders with alacrity. The only thing he volunteered about his background was that his name was not Boot and his accent indicated that he came from somewhere in New England. Then, one day, a little less than two years after he had been admitted, he vanished. He had become so unobtrusive that no one missed him between breakfast and the customary bunk check at night. No one ever saw him again.

Immediately after his disappearance, there was a remarkable transformation in Pearl Hart. Her whole personality changed. She became quiet, soft spoken, and she asked Mrs. Ingalls if she could have a dress and some cosmetics. Shortly after this favor was granted, she asked if she could see a minister. One of Yuma's leading clergymen came to the jail and was closeted with the once-arrogant Pearl Hart for more than an hour.

"She is remorseful over her sins," the cleric told Ingalls. "I think she was still under the influence of this man Boot and now that he has escaped she realizes the error of her ways."

Another six months passed. The minister came to visit her regularly. No longer did Pearl call out lewd invitations to the male prisoners. She asked for books, which Ingalls brought to her, and she began to write poetry. The minister told Ingalls that he thought justice would best be served if Pearl were pardoned and released to the custody of her parents in Kansas City.

"Only the governor can do that," Ingalls explained.

The clergyman wrote to Governor Nathan O. Murphy. About six weeks later, Governor Murphy was in Yuma and he paid a visit to the Arizona Territorial Prison. During his tour, he asked about the prison's female prisoner and Ingalls told him of the remarkable change in Pearl Hart.

"I would like to see her," the governor said.

Ingalls accompanied the governor to the cell. "Let me talk to her alone," Murphy said.

A half hour later, the governor left the prison, telling Ingalls that he would think about a pardon. "I think she was mesmerized by this wretch Boot," the governor said. "She will probably be better off if she is sent back to her family."

Ingalls agreed. So far as he was concerned the prison also would be a lot better off if Pearl Hart were no longer around. He waited for two months for some response from the governor's office, but no word was forthcoming and Ingalls did not feel it would be proper to remind the governor of his previously expressed sentiments.

A guard came to see him while he was pondering the problem. Pearl Hart was ill and would like to see a doctor.

"What's wrong with her?"

The guard shrugged. "She just told me through the bars that she wanted to see a doctor."

Ingalls sent for a nurse from Yuma. "She appears to be pregnant," the nurse told Ingalls a few hours later. "She has all the symptoms."

Ingalls shuddered violently. There were only two keys to Pearl's cell, one in his possession and the other in his wife's. Only two persons had ever been alone with her in the cell: Yuma's leading clergyman and the governor of the Territory.

"How far along is she?" he asked the nurse.

"She has missed twice," the nurse replied delicately.

The superintendent made a command decision. He sent an aide to the railroad station to buy a one-way ticket for Pearl to Kansas City and then, with two guards and a shocked Mrs. Ingalls accompanying him, he went to Pearl's cell. "Your pardon has come through," he said. "You'll be leaving on the train tomorrow." He next went back to his office and wrote a long confidential letter to Governor Murphy and, among other recommendations, he suggested the pardon be dated back a few days.

According to the Yuma *Sentinel*, a large crowd was at the Yuma depot the following day to witness the departure of the "notorious Pearl Hart."

34

"What are you going to do now, Pearl?" a reporter asked.

"I'm going into vaudeville. I've already got a year-long booking as a real-life ex-con and real-life robber."

"Are you going to meet John Boot?"

"You're a stupid bastard," Pearl said mildly, then she waved to the crowd as the train pulled away.

As near as can be determined, no one ever heard from her again.

A few years after Pearl's departure, in 1909, the notorious Yuma prison was abandoned in favor of more modern facilities at Florence. The buildings gradually became ruins and as the decay advanced, the prison became a haven for hoboes. Eventually the hoboes became such a nuisance that the more solid citizens of Yuma started a drive which successfully turned the prison into a museum.

No one today is quite certain which cell was the one used by Pearl Hart. Before the train carrying her was out of Arizona, Ingalls had restored the original six tier bunks and filled the cell with more reliable inmates of the male species.

THE LOST PAYROLL AT WICKENBURG

Late one Sunday morning, November 5, 1871, a stagecoach with eight persons aboard left the small town of Wickenburg, Arizona, for the continuation of a trip that originated in Prescott, Arizona, and was scheduled to terminate in San Bernardino, California. About nine miles outside of the town, six of the eight persons on board were slain in one of the most puzzling mass murders in the history of the Southwest. Before the case was considered closed, at least one hundred more persons had been killed and any discussion of the case today in the Wickenburg area still is a point of controversy.

What is even more ironic is that the two survivors of the

36

massacre most probably were the murderers, yet they were acclaimed as heroes. One mysteriously disappeared a few months after the murders and the other most probably met a violent death a year later.

At first glance, it appeared that the stage had driven into an ambush. Stagecoach holdups during this era were not unusual, but the killing of the passengers and the driver was rare. On board the stage were Mollie Shepherd, a beautiful working madam from Prescott; William Kruger, chief clerk cashier of the Army Quartermaster Corps in Arizona; Fred W. Shoholm, a Prescott jeweler; W. D. Salmon and P. M. Hamel, both members of an Arizona military expedition headed by Lieutenant George Wheeler; C. S. Adams, a rich San Francisco businessman; Frederick W. Loring, writer, poet, and journalist for the New York *Tribune*; and "Dutch John" Lentz, the driver, who was making his first trip for the company.

The two survivors were Mollie Shepherd and William Kruger. The latter was on assignment from the Army to carry approximately $100,000 of Army payroll funds from Arizona to San Bernardino, money which was carried in a large iron box in the back of the stage. In addition to being a cashier for the Quartermaster Corps, Kruger also was Mollie's financial adviser and lover. Shortly before leaving Prescott, Mollie had sold her bordello for a reported $40,000 and she carried this money with her in a small "safe box" which she kept between her feet inside the stage.

The descriptions of both Mollie and Willie are vague. Mollie was believed to be in her early thirties; every reference to her describes her as buxom and beautiful and she had a reputation for "being very close with a dollar." No one ever could recall her buying anyone a drink in her palace of pleasure in Prescott. Willie was known to be short and stocky, in his late thirties, and a man with above-average strength.

37

The stagecoach was "ambushed" in the bottom of a large arroyo. It was not a good location for an ambush. There was only one small tree and three or four small mesquite bushes about a foot tall behind which a killer could hide. There were no rocks that could afford cover. About three quarters of a mile to the south was a small canyon that divided two small foothills. In every other direction was the flat high mesa extending for many miles.

The first to learn of the massacre, other than those aboard the stage, was a young man named Nelson, who was driving a buckboard along the trail several miles to the west when he came upon Mollie and Kruger. Both were disheveled. Mollie was suffering from a bullet burn on her arm and Kruger had a flesh wound in his shoulder. The horrified Nelson did not waste much time to listen to their story. Driving his buckboard into a cover of brush, he told Mollie and Kruger to wait inside it, then unhitched his horse and galloped to the Vulture Mine, about seven miles distant, where he enlisted an armed escort to accompany him into Wickenburg. Here, a twenty-five-man posse was formed which proceeded directly to the ambush site, arriving there shortly before dark.

The lead horse of the stagecoach was dead, but oddly, the other horses still grazed in the area, unhitched from the coach, but still in harness. The bodies of the victims were strewn around the north side of the stage and one, that of P. M. Hamel, had been scalped. All of the trunks and valises had been torn from the coach and smashed open, but no attempt had been made to search them. Wrapped in a shirt in Adams' valise was more than eight thousand dollars. A smaller amount of money and some jewelry were found in Shoholm's suitcase. A sack of mail had been slashed open with a sharp knife and every letter in it which was addressed to the Army Quartermaster Corps had been opened. All of the other mail was sealed and scattered on the ground among the corpses. The stage was riddled with bullet holes on all four sides. No clothing had been taken, no blankets "nor party colored rugs nor gay shawls." All of this puzzled the posse because marauding Indians invariably took horses, harnesses, blankets, and rugs. Missing, however, was the iron box with approximately $100,000 of Quartermaster payroll funds destined for California disbursement. Also missing was the stage shovel.

Because of the encroaching darkness, the posse split up. A dozen made camp near the scene and the remainder went on to rescue Mollie and Kruger from their refuge in the buckboard. It was close to midnight by the time the two survivors were brought back to the posse's camp.

Kruger told a harrowing story. Adams had been riding outside with Lentz. The others rode inside the stage with drawn curtains, "warming themselves with wit, wine, and humor" and playing a game of "freeze-out" on one of Mollie's shawls spread across their knees. Suddenly Dutch John cried out, "Apache," and a split second later the stage was riddled with rifle fire. The volley was fired from the front, the right side and the rear of the stagecoach. Some of the passengers were wounded in the first volley, which accounted for the blood inside the vehicle. Then all but Mollie and Kruger reacted in an incredible manner. They jumped out of the right side of the coach directly into the rifle fire of the attacking Indians and were shot down. Mollie and Kruger however "kept their wits about them." They leaped from the left side of the bullet-riddled stage and ran across the high, flat mesa to the distant canyon.

Their escape did not go undetected. About nine of the savages saw them and set off in pursuit, firing at them with their rifles, but Kruger "kept them at bay by shouting and firing and brandishing my pistol." The Indians chased the two survivors until they reached the sanctuary of the canyon. Here, the Indians

39

fired a few desultory shots after their quarry, then returned to the stage. It was Willie Kruger who told the posse that the Quartermaster payroll funds were missing. Also gone was $40,-000, Mollie's life savings that she had garnered from her palace of pleasure in Prescott.

Additionally, Krueger also told a story about W. D. Salmon that so incensed the posse that its members did not consider it worth the effort to bring this corpse into Wickenburg on the following day. A shallow grave was dug on the site for the remains of Salmon.

On Monday, the posse once again divided. Some accompanied the two survivors to Camp Date Creek, several miles to the north, where there was an Apache reservation and a military encampment. The remainder returned to Wickenburg with the bodies of the victims, except for Salmon's, left at the site. A coroner's inquest was held the following morning and after listening to the testimony from some members of the posse, it issued a verdict that the victims died of gunshot wounds "received at the hands of Indians trailed toward their Date Creek Reservation." (One of the members of the jury was Julius Goldwater, owner of the stage and progenitor of Senator Barry Goldwater.)

A couple of days after the inquest, Captain Charles Meinhold arrived in Wickenburg from Fort McDowell. Meinhold served in what was then the equivalent of the Army Intelligence Corps. He was a small man of thin face and curious mind. He had the habit of swinging his gold-rimmed spectacles loosely in his hand whenever he interrogated anyone. He first asked to see the bodies of the victims, but this was impossible. They had all "been given a good Christian funeral" shortly before his arrival and interred in a local cemetery, with the exception of Salmon. Meinhold, who knew Shoholm, wondered how well his Jewish friend would have appreciated the religious ceremony.

The stage had been returned to Wickenburg and Meinhold found it outside the local blacksmith shop. It was riddled with bullet holes and there was so much blood inside of the coach that he wondered how anyone would have had the strength to leap out. Surely, at least one or two of the passengers would have been mortally wounded by such a fusillade. It was indeed remarkable that anyone could have got out of the stage. There were no bullets left inside the stage. Either they had lodged in the bodies of their victims or passed on through.

There was another odd piece of evidence, also. Bullets had been fired into the coach from the front, the right-hand side and the rear. This would indeed be a hazardous crossfire for Indians to have set up. Those firing from the front quite easily could have hit one of their comrades firing from the rear. At the same time, those firing from the rear could have killed their friends in the front of the stage. Yet it appeared that some of the bullets had entered the front of the stagecoach and splintered in a straight line out of the rear. The same trajectory also was true from the rear of the coach. It did not make sense. If the coach was to be ambushed, "why weren't the Indians shooting from both sides of the trail and why didn't they fire at an angle just before the coach reached them, or immediately after it had passed."

The following day, Meinhold rode out to the scene of the massacre. Here he marveled that so many Indians could have hidden under such sparse cover. True, they could have brought along tumbleweed or mesquite for camouflage, but it was unlikely that they would have carried the weeds away after the massacre. Here the trail followed a dry river bottom in the center of a high mesa. To the south, the ground rose slowly for about three quarters of a mile, where there was a small range of mountains. It was across this long open stretch that Willie Kruger and Mollie Shepherd had fled to reach the sanctuary of the small canyon. Armed with a revolver, Kruger had held back nine

Apaches carrying rifles. Any reasonable marksman with a rifle could have safely picked off a man armed with a short-range revolver in such open country.

Meinhold slowly began to walk in a spiral from the scene of the ambush. About three hundred yards to the north of the site, he found the stagecoach shovel wedged between two rocks. He looked closely for any signs of digging, but the ground was hard clay and could find none. A half-mile to the south of the site, he came across some human feces which contained beans. Beans were a staple diet of reservation Indians, as they were also of Mexicans and most prospectors. He had no way of telling how long the feces had been there. A half-mile from here, the ground became sandy and he found a pack of playing cards similar to those used by both Indians and Mexicans. There were some moccasin tracks. Finally, after he could find nothing more of interest, he rode on to Camp Date Creek, taking the cards and the shovel with him.

Willie Kruger and Mollie Shepherd were resting in separate rooms in the military hospital. Their wounds were far less serious than Meinhold had been led to believe. Mollie was suffering from a bullet burn across the bicep of her right arm. Kruger's left shoulder had been furrowed by a bullet.

Meinhold interviewed them separately. Basically their stories were the same as told to the posse, but there were a few variances.

"How were the Apaches dressed?" he asked Kruger.

"In the blue denim pants and shirts they are given in the reservation," Kruger replied.

He asked the same question of Mollie.

"They were wearing those long Army greatcoats they give them on the reservation," Mollie said.

"Who jumped out of the stage first, you or Mr. Kruger?"

"Mr. Kruger jumped out, then lifted me down."

Meinhold went back to Kruger. "We both jumped out together," Kruger said.

The intelligence officer suggested to the commanding officer of the hospital that the two survivors were not to be released prematurely and then returned to Fort McDowell, where he wrote a report on the results of his investigation to his superior officer, Colonel Nathan Dudley. The colonel added a few notes to Meinhold's report, pointing out the evidential conflicts, and forwarded this on to the bucolic General George Crook, the Commanding General of the Army in the Territory.

There was a peculiar political situation existing in Arizona at this time. When the white settlers first came to Arizona, they were welcomed by the Apaches, but this friendliness was not of long duration. Pioneers appropriated land that the Apaches felt belonged to them and the Indians retaliated by murdering the whites and burning down their farms. The pioneers then called upon the Army for protection and, as anywhere, when the military forces were escalated in Arizona, the hostilities increased in direct proportion. Maintenance of the military also proved profitable to merchants, freight haulers, and contractors.

The slaughter on both sides eventually reached such proportions that a strong reaction swept through the East and Washington for some alternative measure to the problem, other than the ineffectual military pacification policy of extermination. The pressure finally became great enough on the White House to cause President Ulysses S. Grant to send Vincent Colyar, of the Bureau of Indian Affairs, to Arizona as his personal representative and with a directive to come up with a solution to the problem.

Colyar was an Indian partisan and despite the vitriolic protests in the Arizona press, he halted Crook's policy of extermination and successfully brought the Apaches into reservations where the government fed and clothed them. The white settlers bitterly fought the Colyar program, contending that the Apaches con-

43

stantly slipped away from the reservations to pillage and loot. Camp Grant, one of the Apache reservations, was attacked by a group of whites and every Apache man, woman, and child within its confines was slaughtered. Many younger women were raped before they were shot. Despite this massacre, however, the Colyar policy continued. A few weeks before the Wickenburg ambush, Colyar thought his program had progressed to such a point that it was safe for him to return to Washington for a personal report to President Grant.

Crook still agreed with the white settlers that Colyar's policy was nonsensical. When he received Meinhold's and Dudley's reports on the ambush, he instantly attributed the "dastardly deed" to the Apaches. He was enough of a political general, however, not to over-react and for a while he did nothing.

Oddly, the press of the Arizona Territory at first was not as convinced that the Apaches were to blame as was General Crook. The Prescott *Miner*, which was the leading newspaper of the day in the Territory, suggested the assassins could have been Apaches, or Mexicans, or Americans disguised as Apaches.

Two months after the attack, Willie Kruger and Mollie Shepherd left the hospital at Date Creek Camp. Both had fully recovered from their wounds, but had remained at the military post "in case their presence was required during the process of the investigation of this tragic incident." Early in January, the couple once again boarded the stage at Wickenburg. Some days later they were accorded a hero's welcome in Los Angeles. The most minute details of their ordeal were printed in the Los Angeles press in the colorful prose of the day. There was no doubt in Willie's and Mollie's minds that the attackers were Apaches. Kruger went into great detail recounting his arduous running gun battle with the bloodthirsty savages as he carried Mollie to the haven of the canyon.

On the East coast, the newspapers were less concerned with Kruger's miraculous escape than they were with continued lawlessness in the Arizona Territory. The New York *Tribune*, which earlier had supported the Colyar policy, now furiously opposed it because of the wanton murder of one of its star reporters, Fred Loring. Another newspaper quoted Crook as saying the ambush would never have occurred "had not my hands been tied" in his campaign to rid the Territory of the Apache menace. Other newspapers picked up the cry. When Colyar's report on the success of his mission was made public, it was greeted with derision by the press and with highly proclaimed skepticism by the politically sensitive bureaucrats in Washington.

During this period, Meinhold had been continuing his investigation of the Wickenburg Massacre, on the orders of Colonel Dudley. He found a prostitute in Prescott who had worked for Mollie up until the sale of the brothel. She reported that Kruger had met with some Mexicans in the brothel a couple of days before the stage departed. Still another friend of Mollie's said that she had been told not to take "that stage on that particular day."

Shortly after Willie and Mollie had departed for Los Angeles, Salmon's body was removed from its burial spot at the massacre site and brought to Wickenburg by the members of the posse who originally had buried it.

The Prescott *Miner* reported: "This humane and benevolent act was done at the insistence of James Grant, mail contractor, and under the direction of Dr. J. Pierson. The bodies of the six murdered men now rest side by side at Wickenburg."

A few weeks later, Kruger was scathingly attacked by the *Miner* for misrepresenting the facts of the burial of Salmon after the Wickenburg Massacre. The paper referred to Willie Kruger as Mollie Shepherd's paramour. It was discussed openly that Kruger had set up the raid with the help of some Mexican bandits.

45

General Crook angrily disagreed. He announced that there was no doubt but what the assassins were Apaches. At the same time, he released a copy of a letter to President Grant which was a scathing attack upon the Colyar Report. According to some sources, the Crook attack was printed in the New York *Tribune* two days before the original letter reached the White House. Although almost three months had passed since the mass murders had taken place and although they had been under constant investigation by the Army, Crook told a *Tribune* reporter, "The Army will immediately conduct an investigation of the murders in an attempt to hunt down the Apaches responsible for this horrendous deed."

In San Diego, the *Union* printed a story which stated that Mexican raiders were bragging about committing the massacre, "relating detail so accurately that those hearing it had no doubt that it was true. Their boast was corroborated by the fact that they left Sonora with clothes to scarcely cover themselves and returned well-clothed and with plenty of money."

This story was picked up by the Los Angeles *News* and elaborated upon. One of the Mexican participants, the newspaper said, was a Ramón Cordova who presently was a prisoner in jail at Phoenix, Arizona. The following night, a band of vigilantes swooped down on the Phoenix jail, kidnapped Cordova and hanged him from the nearest tree.

Again General Crook issued a statement that the Apaches were solely responsible, chiding the Western press for not agreeing and not rallying public support to combat the Apache menace, as their fellow journalists were doing in the Eastern part of the nation. He implied again, also, that if he were not held back by Washington, he could solve the problem within the matter of a few weeks.

Colonel Nathan Dudley disagreed. As the white settlers began to follow General Crook's cue, Dudley wrote to the Bureau of Indian Affairs: "I do not believe there was an Apache near the scene of the murder. All honest men have the same opinion, if they dared express it."

Reporters in San Francisco found Willie Kruger living in a suite at the Barbary Hotel and asked him to comment on the controversy. "It was Apaches," Willie insisted. "There can be no doubt about it. I saw them and I battled them for hours."

"Are you still in the Army?"

"No, I have been discharged honorably."

"How are you living?"

"From my investments."

"Where is Mollie Shepherd?"

Willie brushed a tear from his eye and the reporter noted that he appeared to have difficulty in answering. Then he raised his head. "She died in Los Angeles a month ago from the wounds inflicted upon her by the savages."

One of the reporters wanted to know why no one had heard of the death before this.

"She asked for a quiet funeral," Willie said. "Of course, I respected her dying wish."

Word of Mollie's death reached the East and no one questioned Willie's version of the passing of his loved one. A San Francisco reporter, however, did, and asked a Los Angeles colleague to get the details. When no record of her death could be found, the reporter went back to the Barbary Hotel. Willie Kruger had moved out. He left no forwarding address.

The New York *Tribune*, still incensed over the death of Loring, continued its attack on the policies of Colyar and the Bureau of Indian Affairs. It demanded in a constant barrage that law and order be restored in the Arizona Territory, asserting that the only way this could be accomplished was to rid the country of Apaches "at once and for all." The outcry was continued by most of the other major newspapers along the northeastern seaboard.

President Grant gave in. He overruled the pacification

policy of the Bureau of Indian Affairs that was instituted by Colyar and ordered General Crook to march against the Apaches.

On September 8, 1872, almost a year after the Wickenburg Massacre, Crook personally led a detachment of troops to the Date Creek Reservation "to arrest those responsible for this foul deed." There has been no explanation ever offered as to why he did not refer the matter to the military detachment which was encamped permanently in an area adjacent to the reservation, nor is there any explanation as to why it did not take part in the ensuing battle.

It was a costly fight. Crook lost a large number of his own men and was almost killed himself, but the toll among the Apaches gathered on the reservation was high, about sixty warriors. A band of fifty Apache warriors escaped.

On September 25, units of the Fifth Cavalry, guided by Hualpai scouts, surprised the band on the Santa Maria River. Forty of the Apaches and a few more soldiers were slain here. After this battle, General Crook announced that the Indians responsible for the Wickenburg Massacre had been found among the dead. "The account is closed," he reported to Washington and the press.

In December of 1872, a short, stocky man, dressed like a prospector, entered a small bar in Phoenix, Arizona, and ordered a straight whiskey. Just as he was about to raise the glass to his lips a gunfight broke out in another part of the room. Two men were killed, one the loser of the altercation and the other, the short stocky man who had just entered the bar.

An investigation, held immediately, disclosed that the winner of the gun battle had acted in self-defense. The prospector had been killed by a stray shot from the other man's revolver. The sheriff went through the stocky man's pockets and found only a few dollars and the key to a nearby hotel room. The man had registered under the name of William Kruger of

San Francisco. He had told the clerk he was planning "a little prospecting" and would be there only one night. There was nothing in his room but some toilet articles and a .38 revolver.

In a nearby livery stable, the sheriff found a mule and horse, purchased the day before by William Kruger, and stored in the stable were camping supplies of the type usually used by a prospector.

No relatives came forward. On the following day, this William Kruger was buried in a common grave. Apparently no one thought to ask if he was the sole survivor of the Wickenburg Massacre.

The $100,000 of federal payroll money in the iron box never has been found and today no one is even certain where the massacre occurred, other than that it is about nine miles west of Wickenburg. No one knows where the old stagecoach trail passed. There is a plaque on Highway 60–70 which runs a few miles south of the old trail which states "somewhere near here is located the Wickenburg Massacre site" and the plaque attributes the murders to the Apaches.

The graves of the victims have become lost. If there ever were any markers placed upon them, they have long since disappeared. There are several dude ranches in the area, including the famed Remuda Ranch. Occasionally a rider from the Remuda will pause near the banks of a dry stream on a high mesa and gaze curiously at a mound of rocks which support a crudely made cross and if, upon his return, he asks its significance, he will be told by Dana Burden, the ranch owner, that it marks the site of Salmon's grave. But Burden will wryly admit that the grave was constructed more than three-quarters of a century after the attack. He will not, however, accept any theory other than that the Apaches were responsible for the murders.

Nevertheless, there was no evidence of any rich Indians around the reservation. If Mexican bandits had strayed that far north of the border, they certainly would not have tarried to bury an empty iron box. But if someone was planning to return to pick up his loot, he would have taken the shovel from the stage and buried the box with its $100,000.

If Willie Kruger was the villain in the Wickenburg Massacre, his plan to get rich cost the lives of some one hundred persons. If the Willie Kruger who was killed in Phoenix was the only survivor of the massacre, then there probably still lies buried $100,000 in one box and about $40,000 of Mollie Shepherd's money in another. It will be somewhere on a high dry mesa, near a dry riverbed, about three quarters of a mile from a small canyon, and about nine miles due west of Wickenburg.

CALIFORNIA'S LOST DIAMONDS

Almost fifty million dollars' worth of raw gold was grubbed from the famed Cherokee Mine of California a few miles north of Oroville. In the late 1870's, the Cherokee was the largest hydraulic gold mine operation in the United States. Under the hydraulic method, huge nozzles called monitors shot high-pressure streams of water against the earth, pulverizing and washing hundreds of tons of it an hour through vast sluice boxes where the heavier gold was separated from the gravel.

The remains of Cherokee today barely accommodate its ghosts, but when the gold mine was in operation, the town contained some seven thousand persons, all of whom were more interested in gold than in diamonds. The first known diamond discovery was made by a gentleman named Mike Maher, who found a perfect blue specimen in 1863. It was considered a freak of nature and no attention was paid to it and the same disinterest prevailed a short time later when John Moore came across a six-carat stone.

The attention of the miners, the merchants, and the prostitutes was focused solely upon gold until 1893, when the California legislature passed an anti-hydraulic mining law which made it impossible for the Cherokee owners to continue operating at a profit. The town died quickly, but itinerant prospectors continued to pick over the tailings.

One of these itinerants was a lean-faced, whiskered gentleman by the name of Jerome Hulsey. Shortly after the turn of the century, Hulsey appeared in a San Francisco bank carrying three large diamonds which he asked to have appraised and placed in a safety deposit vault. This was precisely the opening step that had been taken by Asbury Harpending a few years earlier when he perpetrated the great diamond hoax by salting a field in Colorado with worthless diamonds.

A representative of the bank replied coldly that the bank was not in the business of appraising diamonds and suggested that he take them to a jeweler for appraisal. The bank would be willing to rent Hulsey a safe deposit box, however, and the bewhiskered prospector thought this was a reasonable attitude for the bank to take. He left, saying that he would be back "if these little agates are worth anything."

An hour later he was back with two of the diamonds and a check from a prominent San Francisco jeweler that paid Hulsey $8000. The prospector placed two diamonds in the safe deposit box and insisted upon taking the money for the check in cash. Hulsey immediately rented a suite at the city's finest hotel, the Palace, where he slept during most of the daylight hours. His evenings were spent whooping it up on the Barbary Coast. In less than a month, he had run through his first $8000.

He returned to the bank, canceled his safe-deposit rental and presumably sold his other two "little agates," but to whom and for how much is unknown. He raised enough money, however, to keep him going for approximately three months at the same standard of living he had enjoyed during the first.

Sometime during the fourth month he was evicted from the Palace for nonpayment of his bill. At about the same time, he approached a San Francisco merchant named Abraham Stein for a grubstake, telling Stein that he knew where several more diamonds could be found. Stein gave Hulsey three hundred dollars which he lost the same evening in a Barbary Coast gambling hall. He went back to Stein, told him what he had done, and asked for another grubstake. This time he told Stein that he had found the diamonds in the area of the old Cherokee Mine, but Stein was unimpressed and turned down Hulsey's invitation to advance another grubstake. Hulsey drifted on and, as near as can be determined, was never seen around San Francisco or Cherokee again.

Several years later, Stein was introduced to William Cooney, a South African diamond expert who was visiting San Francisco. During the ensuing conversation, Stein mentioned his experience with Hulsey. Cooney immediately became interested, so much so that he went to Cherokee. He found that the area abounded in kimberlite, a blue volcanic clay contingent with diamonds. He was so impressed that upon his return to San Francisco, he prevailed upon Stein and three other locally prominent financiers to incorporate the United States Diamond Company under the laws of Arizona, with a capitalization of 2.5 million dollars. The stock sold for one dollar a share, with half offered for public sale and the balance reserved for the five founders of the corporation.

Cooney had a flair for publicity. Two days after the stock

was offered for sale, a woman near Cherokee found a two-carat diamond in the craw of the turkey she was cleaning. The stock doubled its value. The corporation took an option on forty acres of land near Cherokee. Three more diamonds were found in the area by Henry Vail, a vice-president of the corporation.

The pattern was closely following the Harpending scandal and one San Francisco newspaper reprinted the story of the great diamond hoax. The price of the stock dropped from three and one half dollars to seventy-five cents, but Stein sold out before it reached its low point and discovered that he had made about three hundred dollars on the deal, which repaid the grubstake he had advanced to Hulsey.

Cooney suddenly became reticent. He shunned reporters, and the United States Diamond Corporation issued no more press releases. When another newspaper hinted broadly that Cooney and Harpending had much in common, Cooney replied tersely that he "didn't give a damn whether anyone bought or sold the stock." He moved his offices from San Francisco to Oroville, although he continued to maintain a luxurious apartment on San Francisco's Nob Hill. Cooney's three remaining partners, including Vail, became nervous and gradually began to unload their holdings in the open market, eventually driving the price down to three cents a share. Visits to San Francisco by Cooney became less frequent.

The city assessor of Chico, California, was a man named Harold Sweetman, who, because of his friendship with Vail, had bought a few thousand shares of the company. One day Sweetman was visited by a smooth-shaven, well-dressed stranger in his forties who spoke English with the same accent as Cooney. The stranger first asked several questions about the tax structure in Chico, implying that he was thinking of building a small manufacturing plant within the city. He then casually brought the subject around to diamonds. Presently he offered to buy Sweetman's shares in the United States Diamond Company. Sweetman said he would think it over and that night he wrote to Vail asking his advice. Vail suggested that he sell, saying that 3 per cent recovery factor was better than nothing. Sweetman followed his advice and sold to the man, who was temporarily living in Oroville.

A couple of weeks later, Vail received another letter, this time from an old friend named Lorbeer who lived in Oroville. Lorbeer told him of a strange happening at the old Cherokee Mine. Two prospectors who had been picking at the tailings of the mine had galloped into Oroville in a state of high excitement. They carried with them a hatful of diamonds encrusted with blue clay—or what they thought were diamonds. The stones had been given to Cooney for appraisal, and Cooney had sent them on to San Francisco for analysis.

Vail sighed, remembering the turkey with the diamond in its craw, and wrote back that Cooney probably was just trying to put some value on worthless stock. Less than a week later, he received another letter from Lorbeer. Another South African was staying with Cooney, and, Lorbeer added, Cooney had announced that the diamonds the miners found were worthless; nothing but shiny rocks. The two miners had objected when Cooney told them he had thrown the rocks away while in San Francisco and Cooney had apologized and given them five-hundred dollars to atone for his oversight. It was at this point that Vail suddenly became suspicious. He recalled the letter from Sweetman and he knew that there were few prospectors who would be able to tell a shiny rock from a diamond when they saw one.

He contacted all of the original partners and discovered that all had sold their stock on the open market. A few days later, he learned that Cooney held almost 90 per cent of the stock in the United States Diamond Company. Furious, Vail went to Oroville to confront the debonair South African.

Cooney readily admitted that he had purchased all of the stock. "It was a humanitarian gesture," he explained. "I felt it was an obligation upon my part to see that these people got back a little something on their investment. After all, it was because of my mistakes that they did make their investment."

"I would like to see the old mine shaft where these so-called rocks were found," Vail demanded.

Cooney shook his head sadly. "It has been boarded up," he explained. "After all, there is no sense in having other people go through the same disappointment."

Vail was nonplussed. He checked before he returned to San Francisco and found that Cooney had, indeed, closed the old mine. But why, if there were diamonds, would Cooney shut down a mine? Conversely, if there were no diamonds, why had Cooney bought up all the stock?

About a month after Vail's visit, Cooney closed up the offices of the United States Diamond Company in Oroville and moved back to San Francisco. Vail was obsessed with finding the answer to the riddle. The more he investigated, the more curious he became. Cooney had exercised the corporation's options on the acreage around the mine. He had paid the taxes on the property, and, if his manner of living in San Francisco was any indication, he was much wealthier than when he had first arrived.

A year went by and Cooney once again paid the taxes on the property. In the spring of the following year, a flash flood after a heavy rain swept through the denuded area.

In the fall of the same year, Vail was in Chico and he stopped in to see his old friend, the city assessor. Inevitably, the subject turned to Cooney and his peculiar behavior.

Sweetman had been paid for his stock in cash. Not once during the two conversations Sweetman had with the purchaser, did the man volunteer his name. He definitely was a foreigner and he spoke English fluently, but with the same accent as Cooney.

A few days after the transaction, Sweetman had been in Oroville and he had seen Cooney and the stranger in the dining room of the Oroville Hotel.

On his way back to San Francisco, Vail detoured by way of the Cherokee Mine. The land was denuded, both from the flood and the hydraulic mining. It was now covered with gravel and debris, and there was nothing resembling the magic blue kimberlite clay. He went to the Oroville Hotel and talked to some of the employees. All remembered the stranger. He had dined on many occasions in the hotel dining room with Cooney during his visit, which was understandable, as he was a guest of the hotel. His name was Schuyler.

Vail asked if he could see the registration ledger.

"Of course," the desk clerk replied.

Jan Schuyler from Johannesburg, South Africa, had been a guest of the hostelry for three weeks. Vail made a note of the address. A few days later, back in San Francisco, he wrote to the mysterious Schuyler.

"Dear Sir," he wrote. "It has come to my attention that you are interested in purchasing stock of the United States Diamond Company. I still have in my possession a few thousand shares of this company which I would be willing to sell to you at a reasonable figure.

"I am aware that you quite probably have not returned to South Africa from California, but I am presuming that your secretary will forward this missive to your present address which, unfortunately, I have misplaced.

"I would be delighted to meet with you anywhere at our mutual convenience to discuss the aforementioned matter."

A little more than two months later, Vail received a reply written on the stationery of the DeBeers Syndicate of Johannesburg. It said that Mr. Schuyler presently was in New York in the United States and that Vail's letter had been forwarded to him.

Vail made a few more inquiries and discovered that the DeBeers Syndicate reportedly controlled 88 per cent of the world's diamond production and that it kept a reserve fund of approximately half a billion dollars, from which it could finance purchase of newly discovered diamond mines throughout the world.

Vail never received a reply from Schuyler. A subsequent letter sent to the DeBeers Syndicate also went unanswered.

For several years after the closing of the mine, Cooney lived as a millionaire in San Francisco. In later years, he lived more conservatively and, in 1922, he moved to Salem, Oregon. Then in 1929, the stock market crash apparently hurt him severely because during the Depression he lived very modestly in Salem. When he died in 1942, at the age of ninety, he was almost a pauper.

The area in which the old mine shaft was located is well known. Cherokee still is carried on California maps, but no one seems to know who, if anyone, has title to the old mine.

HENRY CRABB A BORN LOSER

The popularity of the filibusterers during the mid-nineteenth century was indeed great in San Francisco. It was here that William Walker raised money and troops for a hapless expedition into Baja California that ended in ignominy when he commandeered some stolen cattle from a Mexican bandit. Because of this, Walker was run back into the United States with his only possession the suit of underwear he was wearing.

Natives of San Francisco spent money as lavishly as a Pentagon general when a filibustering expedition was involved, raising the funds effortlessly on the presumption that the filibusterer was going to liberate the Mexicans. No one ever did quite understand why the Mexicans never gave a damn about being liberated.

After William Walker came a gentleman by the name of Gaston Rausset de Boulbon, who said he was a French count, but who was definitely one of the finest French chefs of the city by the Golden Gate. Boulbon replaced his tall white hat with a duck-billed cap one day in 1852 and declared himself the governor-general and military dictator of the Mexican State of Sonora.

Generous San Franciscans quickly raised enough money to buy Boulbon a brig named the *Challenge*, with enough left over to finance and supply an army of three hundred. A few weeks later, the *Challenge* dropped anchor at the harbor of Guaymas. The first detachment to land was greeted by an army of four hundred Mexican soldiers, under command of a General Yañez. Forty-eight of the count's army were killed and seventy-eight were wounded. The count was brought before a Mexican military court that convened on the beach, found guilty of fili-bustering, and executed. The remainder of his army, still on board the *Challenge*, decided to return to San Francisco. They were only a few miles out of the harbor, however, when the ship was capsized by an extraordinarily large tidal bore sweeping up the Gulf of California, which effectively wiped out the remainder of the Boulbon liberation expedition.

Five years passed before the next attempt was made to liberate Sonora. Unlike the others, the idea for this expedition was originated in Sonora by experts in the art of chicanery. They picked their victim well: a handsome and fairly young dilettante from San Francisco who was thoroughly fed up with the illiterate masses in California and the so-called democratic procedures in the United States.

His name was Henry A. Crabb. He was the son of a rich Southern farmer who had made a fortune dealing in slave traffic. Shortly after achieving majority, Crabb moved to San Francisco.

With the help of his father, he financed a half-dozen small businesses in San Francisco, none of which took much of his time, but all of which proved successful. He liked to entertain and to deliver polemics on the role of the Negro in the new society of the United States so it was natural that he would gravitate to politics. He served one term in the California State Assembly, but was defeated when he ran for reelection. He next ran for the United States Senate as a candidate for the Know-Nothing Party. Again, he was defeated. It was after this that he began to complain seriously about the emergence of the lower classes in the United States as a political force.

Shortly after his arrival in San Francisco, Crabb had married a beautiful young Mexican aristocrat named Filomena Ainsa, a direct descendant of the well-known Spanish explorer, Juan Bautista de Anza. Her father was Don Manuel Ainsa, who, although he was eminently successful in business in San Francisco, was a very bitter man because all of his holdings in Sonora had been confiscated. He, too, objected to the emergence of the lower classes as a political power, not only in the United States, but in Mexico as well.

When Don Manuel was very young, Augustine de Iturbide had proclaimed himself Emperor of Mexico. Iturbide had the support of the Ainsas, along with most of the rest of the Mexican aristocracy. Very shortly after he assumed power, however, the regime was challenged by a revolutionary named Vincente Guerrero and Guerrero won the support of the state government officials in Sonora. The mine-owners shut down their mines in protest. The landowners let their land lie fallow. In retaliation, the state government confiscated all of the Ainsa properties as a warning to other aristocrats. Manuel Ainsa fled to the United States with his parents.

The other members of the aristocracy in Sonora fought back by financing a local revolution against the state government, a revolution which they won. They then declared their support of the distant Emperor Iturbide. The Ainsas returned to Sonora, happily, to reclaim their property; then left sadly when they discovered their former friends had divided it among themselves because the Ainsas had not remained to help in the revolt. Eventually, Iturbide was overthrown, but the new federal government did not think it worth the effort to replace the conservative state government in isolated Sonora and this conservative element still ruled the state when Boulbon and Walker made their abortive attempts to "liberate" it.

Manuel Ainsa had a close friend in Sonora named Hilario Gabilondo. Like Ainsa, Gabilondo came from a proper family, and like Ainsa, his family had lost considerable holdings to the state government which was controlled by Governor Jesus Gandera. There was still another man who had felt the confiscatory hand of Gandera. His name was Ignacio Pesqueira and he had fled to the hills to attempt the organization of a peasant army which would overthrow Gandera. Unfortunately, Pesqueira had no arms, no money, and such a small handful of followers that Gandera did not think it important enough to send General Yañez after him.

The voyage from Sonora to San Francisco is not a long one and Hilario Gabilondo made frequent trips to the California city. Usually, he was either a house guest of Crabb's or Ainsa's. On his trip in December, 1856, he was the guest of Ainsa. It was on this trip that he proposed to his host that Ainsa and Crabb finance a shipment of arms to Pesqueira and also lend him a sufficient amount of money to overthrow the corrupt government of Gandera. In return for this relatively minor investment, Gabilondo proposed, Ainsa would have all of his former holdings restored. Crabb would be given a large grant of land and, additionally, the authority to operate some of the more productive mines in the area.

"But Pesqueira is nothing more than a peasant," Ainsa protested.

"He can be handled all the more easily," Gabilondo replied. "Once he is in power, we will make him feel like an aristocrat and he will do as we want."

The following day, Gabilondo and Ainsa went to see Crabb. The frustrated politician was indeed interested. He told Gabilondo how disgusted he was with the stupidity of the California electorate. The idea of the good life of a Mexican aristocrat in Sonora appealed to him. An agreement was drawn up and signed by Crabb and by Gabilondo, the latter identifying himself as a bona fide agent of Pesqueira. In return for a shipload of rifles and ammunition and $10,000 of United States currency, Crabb was to be given 400,000 acres of good farmland and a franchise to operate at least two of the more productive silver mines for a period of ninety-nine years. As soon as Pesqueira was in power, Crabb would come to Sonora.

In addition, Crabb wanted the agreement signed by Pesqueira so that there would be no misunderstanding. Gabilondo protested, but Crabb was insistent.

Two months later, Gabilondo was back in San Francisco. Pesqueira had signed the contract and as soon as Pesqueira was in control of the government, Crabb would be given a royal welcome on his arrival in Sonora.

A few weeks after this, a ship anchored offshore somewhere between Guaymas and Hermosillo to unload a large shipment of arms and ammunition for Pesqueira. Presumably, the $10,000 in cash also was given to Pesqueira through Gabilondo, to allow him to finance the recruitment of an army of his own. The revolution that overthrew Gandera and sent him and General Yañez to refuge in Mexico City was extremely short. The federal government in the Mexican capital was pleased over the outcome because it wiped out the last pocket of Iturbide supporters. If anyone in the capital wondered where Pesqueira acquired his strength, the question was not raised publicly.

As soon as word of Pesqueira's success reached San Francisco, a jubilant Crabb mapped his plans for his foray into Mexico. Ninety men were recruited immediately for an overland trip to Sonora. General John D. Cosby was retained to raise another thousand "volunteers," who would then proceed by ship to Port Lobos on the Sonoran coast and rendezvous with Crabb's advance party in the vicinity of Altar, Mexico. Some of these men would be placed in government positions; others would have managerial positions on the hacienda or at the mines. All would become rich. Crabb made no mention publicly of the concessions he had been granted by Pesqueira and the San Francisco newspapers gleefully reported the expedition as another filibustering foray. The Mexican consul general, Don Luis del Valle, forwarded copies of the newspapers to Mexico City. Others wound up in the possession of Jesus Gandera and General Yañez in Mexico City. Before Crabb departed from San Francisco in January of 1857, Mexican newspapers in the capital, Guadalajara, and Vera Cruz were angrily denouncing the start of still another filibuster by American bandits. The Mexican federal government sent a courier to Hermosillo to see if Pesqueira was adequately equipped to withstand the expected invasion. The courier reported back that Pesqueira had a force of more than twenty-five hundred men equipped with the latest American rifles, plus ammunition, and even three mobile cannons. His army, the courier said, was better equipped than the best troops in the federal forces.

Crabb assumed the title of general, bid farewell to his wife and four-year-old son, Augustin, and sailed with a division of ninety men from San Francisco to Los Angeles. Among the ninety was Jesus Ainsa, his brother-in-law, who was to act as interpreter. The advance contingent paused in El Monte, a suburb of Los Angeles, to outfit the expedition, then headed overland toward the arduous Camino del Diablo to Mexico. Why Crabb chose this tortuous overland route in place of a quicker and more comfortable sea voyage is a mystery that never has been explained, other than that Crabb was destined to be as poor a general as he was a politician. The expedition was plagued with trouble even before it had completed the comparatively easy stage of the journey between El Monte and Yuma. Men became sick from drinking bad water. Others were injured in accidents. One of the covered wagons that had been purchased collapsed a little more than fifty miles out and had to be abandoned along with supplies for which there was no room in the other wagons.

In San Francisco, General Cosby suddenly lost all interest in the expedition. He made no attempt to recruit the additional thousand men, nor to buy the ship and supplies. Men who did apply to join the task force were turned away. One report tells that the general moved into more luxurious quarters on Nob Hill and invested heavily and successfully in the stockmarket.

In Mexico City, Gandera and General Yañez managed to get copies of the report made by the federal government courier and both speculated publicly that Pesqueira had received his arms from Crabb and that he planned to turn the State of Sonora over to the filibusterers as part of the deal. Pesqueira was incensed. There was not a bit of truth to the charge, he cried. To prove it, he issued a manifesto calling upon all Sonorans to take up arms in defense of their homeland and drive out the filibusterers.

In the latter part of March, Crabb reached the small border town of Sonoita. His forces of ninety had dwindled to sixty-nine. The casualties had been left behind in small towns to recover and of the sixty-nine, twenty-nine were in such poor health that Crabb decided to leave them behind to rest and follow the main expedition at a more leisurely pace. It was in Sonoita that Crabb learned for the first time that all was not going well in Sonora. While camped just across the border, he was greeted by an emissary of Don Jose Maria Redondo's, the prefect of Altar, a city a few miles into Mexico, who stated that if Crabb entered the State of Sonora he would be annihilated by the armed forces of the state.

Now Crabb was incensed. He wrote a stinging letter to

Redondo, pointing out that he was coming at the invitation of some of the most influential persons in the state and warning Redondo that if any blood was shed, Redondo would have to bear the full blame. He told the messenger, also, that he would be glad to receive Redondo and explain the situation to him when he arrived in Caborca, where he was to rendezvous with nine hundred other men arriving by sea. Then, with forty men at his side, General Henry Crabb marched into Mexico.

In Hermosillo, Pesqueira greeted the news of the invasion by issuing another manifesto urging his fellow Sonorans to "rise and repulse the pirates." He then appointed Hilario Gabilondo as commander-in-chief of the Sonoran forces and Gabilondo dispatched a military detachment of 250 soldiers to Caborca with orders to ambush Crabb. The detachment consisted of one officer, Captain Lorenzo Rodriguez, and 249 enlisted men. Few, including Rodriguez, had ever been in a fight.

Rodriguez chose Caborca as the site of the ambush. He lined up his men in the cover of a large wheat field immediately outside of the old city's limits. On the morning of April 1, General Crabb and his army of forty men arrived in the outskirts of Caborca. When the first fusillade failed to bring down any of the enemy, Captain Rodriguez suddenly realized that he had positioned his men too far distant from the invaders to ensure any accurate fire. Standing up, he led his men in a charge, but as soon as he got within range of the Crabb forces, he was shot and killed. His detachment immediately retreated into the city.

There was a slight skirmish as Crabb entered the city, but within a very short time, the Mexican detachment took refuge in the Catholic church and the invaders requisitioned a large adobe house across the plaza from the church. For the rest of the day, the battle was a Mexican standoff, both sides firing in a desultory fashion at the other, but with no casualties inflicted.

The following day, Crabb decided to attack the convent

that abutted the church. Fifteen men, including Crabb, made the dash across the plaza. Eleven of them reached their objective. Once the convent was captured, Crabb decided to blow down the main connecting door to the church. A keg of powder was placed against the base of the door, but the "slow match" was damp and the powder could not be exploded. Crabb then wrote a note to the remaining men in the adobe house on the other side of the plaza asking that they send over another "slow match." A small Mexican girl who had been hiding in the convent was asked to take the note across. She agreed to undertake the chore, but apparently after leaving the convent she forgot her mission, for a new "slow match" never arrived.

For the next two days, nothing happened, other than that one Mexican soldier was shot while attempting to raise a Mexican flag over the belfry of the church. Then early in the morning of the next day, Crabb heard a commotion in the plaza, with cries of "Viva Don Hilario Gabilondo." General Crabb sighed with relief. One of his influential friends had arrived and apparently had the confidence of the Caborca citizenry. General Crabb raised a white flag of truce. Accompanied by one of his men, he stepped out of the convent.

J. Y. Ainsa tells of the next sequence of events in a small, privately published pamphlet printed in Phoenix, Arizona, in 1951.

As the two invaders came out of the convent, armed men began appearing in the plaza, although none came near and no one spoke. Crabb and Byven, one of his aides, walked down the street toward where they could hear the hails for Gabilondo and finally, after wending their way through several narrow streets, came out onto a large corral containing approximately one hundred saddled horses. Adjacent to the corral was an adobe building with a long veranda, crowded with armed men. At the end of the veranda, speaking to the men, was General Crabb's

67

friend, Gabilondo. Joyfully, Crabb pushed his way toward him.

"Don Hilario, my friend," he said holding out his hand. "It is a pleasure to see you."

Gabilondo gave no sign of recognition. "Who are you?" he asked harshly.

Crabb looked at him in amazement. "You do not know me?" he asked. "You do not know the man to whom you granted all the concessions and whose money you have taken?"

Gabilondo waited for no more. Lifting a sword from a table, he swung it in an arc. Before Crabb could realize what was happening, his head was partially severed from his body. Gabilondo then ordered that the unconscious General Crabb be dragged from the porch and the decapitation completed. Byven was taken prisoner and upon orders of someone other than Gabilondo, was immediately taken away by a six-man detachment to Altar.

In the plaza, meanwhile, the nine men left in the convent slowly came out into the open, following the example of their general. Two of the armed Mexicans in the square drifted behind them, looked inside the convent, saw that it was empty, and then one of them signaled. The nine men were instantly shot where they stood. Many of the assailants then were cut down by a fusillade of bullets from the opposite side of the plaza by the remainder of Crabb's forces.

The fight was about over, however. Within the next couple of hours, the Gabilondo army successfully set fire to the thatched roof of the adobe house. The defenders attempted unsuccessfully to put out the fire by blowing up gunpowder. By dusk, they had to choose between surrender or incineration; they chose the former, but their lives were prolonged by only a matter of minutes. After all had surrendered their arms, they were marched over to the corral and all but one were shot. The exception was a sixteen-year-old youth named Charles Edward

Evans, who was imprisoned for about six months, then sent back to the United States.

A few days later, a Gabilondo patrol intercepted the second contingent of Crabb's forces, a twenty-man group, and killed them all. The patrol then went on to Sonoita, crossed the border and killed the ill and the sick who had been left there, with one exception, Jesus Ainsa, who was taken prisoner. Ainsa, Evans, and Byven all were released and returned to the United States. Jesus Ainsa, however, returned very shortly to Sonora where he was granted land and mining concessions, only to have them expropriated some years later when still another revolution resulted in a new party in control of the government.

In Guaymas today, there is a statue of General Yañez, who defeated the filibusterer Boulbon. In Caborca, the date that marked the death of Crabb is celebrated as an annual holiday because he is thought of in Mexico as a hated filibusterer, rather than as a vain and rather foolish man who was the victim of a most elaborate swindle. Pesqueira governed for many years in Sonora and Gabilondo died a wealthy and respected man, as did General Cosby in San Francisco.

The head of General Crabb was displayed in a large bottle of mescal in Caborca for many years, then it, too, became lost.

A LOST CHORD IN TIJUANA BRASS

Telegrams come and telegrams
  go
Over the wires to Mexico
Ferris the bold, is keeping them
  hot
But Diaz the diplomat answers
  not
  —*San Francisco Chronicle*

The decimation of Henry Crabb's party proved a successful deterrent to other would-be filibusterers and Mexico was left pretty much alone by North American invaders, until the start of the twenty-four-year-long revolution in Mexico that followed the ouster of the Dictator Porfirio Diaz in 1912. General John Pershing spent 130 million dollars in his futile chase of Pancho Villa around the desolate deserts of Chihuahua, after Villa raided

70

Columbus, New Mexico. At about the same time there was an incursion into Baja California by a peculiar assortment of Wobblies—soldiers of fortune, dedicated and mercenary Mexicans loosely united under the banner of a Mexican presidential contender named Ricardo Flores Magon. For several years, this ragtail army of Magon's lived in the northern part of Baja California in a state of utter confusion because of Magon's reluctance to leave his Los Angeles hideout and, even more, because of the antics of a California press agent and promoter known as Ferris the Bold.

Richard Wells Ferris made his first public appearance as an actor in Washington, D.C. He moved to Los Angeles in 1867 where he continued as an actor. He married a well-known actress named Florence Stone and for several years they appeared in popular plays together, both in San Francisco and in Los Angeles. By 1910, he had become expert enough in fooling the public that he decided he was well qualified for politics. He ran, as a Democrat, for the lieutenant-governorship of California. Out of the 100,000 votes cast, Ferris lost by only 6,000. Immediately after the election, he had plans for running for public office again and decided that it would improve his image if he temporarily gave up his acting career. Through political friends, he was appointed director of publicity for the Panama-California Exposition, a year-long fiesta to be held in San Diego's sprawling Balboa Park.

"You can count on me to dream up some live publicity stunts which will hold the public's attention indefinitely," he promised the Exposition's commissioners. The commissioners nodded in approval, although it is unlikely that any of them knew what Ferris had in mind. Certainly Ricardo Flores Magon had no idea that the revolution he was setting up in Baja was due to become demoralized because of the activities of a San Diego press agent.

71

Magon's role in fomenting dissent against the Diaz regime has been well chronicled by historians. An avowed anarchist, he had been fighting Diaz since 1900, when he founded the newspaper *La Regeneración* in Mexico City. Forced to flee to the United States, he continued to publish the paper, first in San Antonio, Texas, then in St. Louis, Missouri, and finally in Los Angeles. It was in St. Louis in 1906 that he planned the first unsuccessful rebellion against Diaz in Chihuahua and Sonora. He tried again in 1908 and failed. Members of his Liberal party were arrested by the thousands in Mexico, despite Diaz' assertion to James Creelman, a reporter for *Pearson's Magazine*, that he would welcome the formation of an opposition party.

By 1911, when Ferris the Bold was hired as publicity director for the Panama-California Exposition, Diaz had a more powerful enemy in the person of Francisco I. Madero, who had formed the Anti-Reelectionist party and whose army had taken possession of the City of Juarez, across from the United States city of El Paso. Magon believed the Maderistas should be subservient to the Liberal party if for no other reason than Magon's seniority in fighting Diaz and thus, in Los Angeles, Magon mapped his plans for the invasion of Baja California. This, he believed, would give him a Mexican base from which he could eventually assume his proper role in the Mexican government. The target for the invasion was Mexicali.

Four Magonistas were contacted in the border city and ordered to recruit supporters, a task that was rather difficult to carry out, as most of the fervid Magonistas were in jail. On the United States side, the assignment of raising a guerrilla army was given to two Mexicans, Jose Maria Leyva and Simon Berthold. Both were active members in the Industrial Workers of the World, better known as Wobblies, who had spent most of their time in Los Angeles exhorting against the labor policies of General Harrison Otis of the Los Angeles *Times*. These two men

72

paused at the Wobblies headquarters in Holtville, picked up four men there, then crossed the border to collect a dozen men who had been recruited there. The sixteen-man army captured Mexicali easily. The only casualty in the early morning raid was the town's jailer, who was shot accidentally while the Magonistas were being released from prison.

When word of the invasion reached the Baja California capital in Enseñada, it was treated casually by the territorial governor, one Colonel Celso Vega. Vega had been appointed by Diaz, but apparently he was of sufficient political bent to wait out the situation calmly until he could determine how the revolution was proceeding on the mainland. Many Mexicans apparently had similar inclinations because there was no immediate uproar in Mexicali over the change in the municipal government. The city's capture, however, did stir up a furor in the United States.

The Wobblies immediately gave their support to Magon and, as most of them were out of work, it was not difficult to expand the army of occupation to approximately 150 men. The army was divided into about even thirds of Wobblies, Mexicans, and Cocopah Indians, and later was augmented by a scattering of mercenaries. It was financed by taxes placed on the merchants and collections made by appeals through Magon's newspaper and money raised by the Wobblies in southern California.

Vega finally decided to run the invaders back across the border. He enlisted an army of 100 volunteers and six regulars and marched toward Mexicali. A few more volunteers arrived from Tijuana and in the town of Tecate, Vega paused for drill practice. Unexpectedly heavy rains slowed the practice sessions and many of the volunteers quietly slipped away. Nevertheless, Vega was able to dislodge a small contingent of Magonistas from Picacho Pass and by mid-February, he set out for Mexicali once again. When his army was passing through a ranch owned by an American named Louis Little, it was ambushed by the

73

Magonistas. Several more of the Vega "volunteers" resigned immediately and Vega was wounded. After a few minutes of fighting, Vega headed back toward Enseñada and, peculiarly, the Magonistas went back to Mexicali.

It was at this point that Ferris the Bold began to take an interest publicly in Baja California. He called a press conference in San Francisco and announced that because Baja California was so close to San Diego, where the Panama-California Exposition was to be held, and because so many visitors would be coming to San Diego, it would be in everyone's best interests if Diaz would sell Baja California to a group of American multimillionaires. He followed this up quickly with a series of announcements that J. P. Morgan and James Hill were interested in the project. The new state would be named the Republic of Diaz and after a brief period of independence, it would be sold to the United States for "a neat profit to the sponsors of the transaction." Ferris then called upon Dr. Plutarco Ornelas, the Mexican consul in San Francisco, with a demand that the proposal be forwarded at once to Diaz for consideration.

A few days later, Ferris announced that if Diaz refused to sell, he would be faced by a Ferris-led filibuster. No sooner did this announcement come out, than ads appeared in the New York *American*, the *World*, and the *Herald* seeking more than one thousand men with a solid military background to join General Dick Ferris. The ads promised to pay all expenses for those found to be qualified.

The Los Angeles *Herald* reported that Ferris planned to operate a sporting republic beyond the border with gambling and the pursuit of pleasure.

Magon paid little attention, nor did his ragtail army, which was still carousing in Mexicali with occasional shootouts and "elections" of commanding officers. The Mexican merchants and professional strata were finally becoming annoyed. The Calexico

Chronicle referred to the Magonistas as "predatory marauders" and the resentment against the enforced tribute to support the band grew daily. Peter B. Kyne, the western novelist, interviewed Rhys Pryce, after he had been elected general, at the commandeered Little Ranch and was told that money collected on the Mexican side of the border had been sent on to Magon in Los Angeles to purchase more arms and ammunition and enlist more men. Magon, according to Pryce, used the money for propaganda, and thus his triumphant army was restricted to a membership of 150 and confined to the Mexicali area. From Los Angeles Magon issued orders which were ignored. He, in turn, ignored repeated suggestions that he come back to Mexico and assume command of his troops, whose mission was to seize control of the entire nation.

During this hiatus, Ferris the Bold was rather inactive in his drive for a separate state in Baja California, probably because he had taken an additional job as press agent for the San Francisco Native Sons Fiesta. As soon as this project was completed, however, Ferris returned to San Diego, picked up a reporter from the *Tribune*, and journeyed to Mexicali to meet with General Rhys Pryce.

"We discussed matters of mutual concern," Ferris said. "It would be premature to disclose the details of the conversation at this time."

Even this meeting prompted only a minor reaction from Magon. He kissed him off with the following comment in his newspaper. "Ferris, the Ferocious Filibusterer, is still making a wee noise like a sporting republic for Baja California. But that noise has become very wee indeed, scarcely more than the feeble peep of a newborn chick."

The Mexican segment of the Magon army in Mexicali began to dwindle. Most of the Mexicans were patriots who had long followed Magon's leadership, but when Magon still refused

75

to return to Mexico, these soldiers switched their allegiance to the more courageous Madero who, on the mainland, was winning his battle against Diaz. Because of these defections, Magon's army now consisted primarily of a group of thugs and Wobblies. Among its officers were Marshall Brooks, a cattle rustler from Campo; Sam Barron, a professional train robber; James Dunham, who had murdered his wife and several of her relatives with an ax in Los Gatos; and Mojave Red, who was reputed to have beaten at least a half-dozen men to death with his huge fists. With additions such as these, Magon's army had increased to about 250 men. Shortly after the visit to Pryce by Ferris the Bold, Pryce took his army on the march. A small segment moved to the south and captured the tiny fishing village of San Quintín without a shot. The main force of the army moved on to Tijuana, about sixteen miles south from the center of San Diego. Neither the defenders nor the attackers of Tijuana had much ammunition. Pryce had been promised a cache of 20,000 rounds from Magon, but once again, Magon had found a more important purpose for the money which had been sent to pay for it. The defenders of Tijuana numbered about 150 and Colonel Vega had failed to send sufficient ammunition to beat back the attack.

Ferris was well aware of the pending battle and from San Diego he proclaimed that the fight would be a safe one for tourists and residents to watch, as there was a notable lack of ammunition on both sides. Visitors thronged by the hundreds to the border and extra United States troops had to be called out to prevent many of the tourists from crossing over into the battle zone. One indignant tourist slugged an American soldier with a bottle of whiskey and was carted off to jail.

Despite the scarcity of ammunition, 32 persons were killed and 24 wounded before Magon's army of the Liberal party captured Tijuana, sending the defenders fleeing either to Ensenada or across the border into political exile in the United States.

There was little for the disgruntled tourists to see, although they could hear occasional rifle shots in the border city.

When the fight was over, Magon claimed the twin victories of Tijuana and San Quintín as outstanding for the Liberal army. Fund-raising rallies were held in Los Angeles to carry on the struggle against the capitalistic robbers in Mexico and one of them was addressed by no less a person than Emma Goldman, the fiery American anarchist. Ferris also approved. He predicted that Tijuana would become the sporting capital of the new republic and that visitors to the Panama-California Exposition would find a side trip to this fun-loving city a delightful experience.

Magon sent an administrator, Antonio de Pio Araujo, to Tijuana to handle civilian affairs and formulate policy for the Liberal party. Pryce and his second in command, Jack Moseby, welcomed Araujo, but ignored his recommendations. Ferris also arrived in Tijuana, accompanied by a reporter from the San Diego *Union*. Again, Ferris and Pryce met secretly, then came out to talk to the newsman. When the reporter asked Pryce if he was working for the Liberal party, Pryce nodded that he was.

Ferris shook his head. "Rhys is too nice a fellow to be mixed up with that bunch," he replied.

Pryce did not bother to contradict Ferris the Bold, and the reporter and promoter once again returned to San Diego. Immediately after their departures, Pryce initiated some civil measures of his own. All tourists coming to Tijuana were to be charged a twenty-five-cent admission fee. Southern California gamblers who wished to provide their own venture capital could open up their own gambling casinos, providing they were agreeable to paying 25 per cent of their gross receipts to the Liberal army of occupation. Faro and poker palaces started immediately and work was begun on an elaborate gambling casino that "will rival Monte Carlo in its grandeur." Within a week the "take" for Pryce's army of occupation was running into hundreds upon hundreds of dollars daily. On two occasions, Pryce sent couriers north to Los Angeles carrying money to Magon. One shipment was for $300, the other for half of this amount. Magon, the great liberal and anarchist, accepted the money and said nothing about Pryce's treatment of Araujo.

In Mexico City, Madero successfully toppled the government of Porfirio Diaz, and the aging dictator fled into exile. Magon accused Madero of offering to sell out to Diaz for 20 million pesos and vowed to continue the struggle, but he still remained in Los Angeles. In Tijuana, Pryce's army grew numerically, but few of its members were Mexicans. There was a steady influx of Wobblies and one, who joined briefly, was the famed IWW troubadour, Joe Hill. Fifty Italian anarchists arrived en masse from the Pacific Northwest and were immediately enlisted. The army's casualty rate was high, not from battle, but from constant fighting among its members. A senior officer named Hopkins found a war chest containing $8,000. He decided upon immediate retirement and crossed the border, taking the money with him. He was last seen boarding the "Owl" train for Los Angeles.

The new government in Mexico City denounced the occupation of Mexicali, San Quintín, and Tijuana as filibustering. Ferris immediately replied that the army of occupation was a genuine republican force and that elections soon would be held to prove that the people of Baja California wanted an independent nation and that any attempt to destroy this new and glorious state would be met valiantly by its united citizens. Pryce went to San Diego for a meeting with Ferris, leaving the town in charge of an "acting general named Tamelyn."

What transpired at this meeting is unknown, but on the following day, Pryce went on to Los Angeles and Ferris went to Tijuana, where he met with Tamelyn and Moseby. After this

78

meeting, the troops that could be found were summoned for an assembly.

"You've got to haul down the red flag," Ferris orated to the group. "While that might mean the symbol of the Liberal party in Mexico, it means anarchy in America. You've got to get that out of sight of every American who passes this border. You've got to cut out socialism, anarchism, and every other ism you've got into." He added that a government would have to be established that would appeal to the American press and "the better class of Mexicans" and by doing this they could get more American money and sympathy.

When the speech was finished, Ferris returned to his Exposition offices in San Diego. A few hours later, the troops once again were assembled by an officer named Louis James. Unfortunately, his rank was not high enough to command the presence of more than seventy-five soldiers and they were anxious to get back to the faro games. They listened to approximately the same exhortation from James as had been given by Ferris a few hours earlier. One of the soldiers walked over to a flagpole and cut the halyards with his machete, then kicked the fallen flag to one side. James then nominated Ferris for president and called for an immediate vote. The count was "seventy-five aye; none for nay." Ferris the Bold had won his second bid for public office overwhelmingly.

James left immediately for San Diego to convey the news to Ferris. "You have just been elected president of Baja California," he announced. "Your people are awaiting you in Tijuana."

"I'm busy today," Ferris replied.

"Well, we need a new flag," James said. "We cut down the old one."

Ferris did have time to design a new flag, one with two horizontal bars across a field of blue with a white star in the

79

center, which he sent to a tailor with orders to have it ready by the following morning. He then called a press conference to announce his election and to say that he was seriously considering acceptance of the office. The new state now would be known as the Republic of Madero, rather than the Republic of Diaz, as originally proposed. He would see that Madero was notified of this new development, Ferris announced, and he would see also that the Mexican government was paid 15 million dollars to cover their costs for the revolution in Lower California.

"What happens if Madero doesn't like it?" a reporter asked.

"He will just have to accept it," Ferris replied.

"What about Flores Magon?"

"We are severing all connections with this junta."

Meanwhile, the Wobblies in the army, who had not bothered to attend the earlier election, held an assembly of their own. During this meeting, Hopkins and Pryce were court-martialed in absentia, the halyards repaired on the flagpole, and the red flag was flown once again over Tijuana. The Wobblies then proceeded to hold an election for a new general, and Jack Moseby defeated his competitor, Paul Schmidt, by twenty votes. Schmidt immediately resigned and left for the United States, where he was arrested for trying to smuggle a Mexican horse across the border. Moseby then sent word to the San Diego *Union* that "Dick Ferris has absolutely nothing to do with the revolutionary movement and his presence in Tijuana is not desired."

Ferris, meanwhile, had gone to Los Angeles with James where, with some friends, they were celebrating his election at a dinner in the plush Alexandria Hotel. While here, he received word that the Wobblies had deposed him as president and elected Moseby as their governing general. Ferris then announced that in order to make his position legal, he would return to Tijuana and run against Moseby in still another election.

James accompanied Ferris as far as San Diego, on his return trip. Here Ferris hired a chauffeur-driven car which, with the flag of the new Republic of Madero flying from a standard on its mudguard and Ferris in the rear seat, set out on its trip to Tijuana from in front of the Exposition offices in San Diego. A short time later, the car sped through customs and into downtown Tijuana. Here it was stopped by the Wobblies, who ripped off the offensive flag, pulled Ferris from the seat, and sent him running for his life back to the border. The following day, the beautiful Mrs. Ferris, accompanied by three friends, arrived in Tijuana as an intermediary between her husband and Moseby, but she found Moseby unsympathetic. He sent her bouncing back across the border without even refunding the dollar admission charge she had been forced to pay when she entered. When she related this unseemly conduct to her husband, he responded by issuing another lengthy statement resigning his presidency. He found that his duties with the Panama-California Exposition were too demanding to participate in the founding of the new republic.

With General Jack Moseby in charge of the occupation army, there was no relationship with Flores Magon and the attempt to justify the invasion as a part of an internal revolution was ludicrous. Moseby put on a Wild West show to attract tourists, but he did not know how to publicize it and no one came. The gambling patronage fell off. He then threatened to blow up a small railroad owned by Adolf Spreckels and a canal works that irrigated property owned by General Harrison Otis unless he was paid approximately $100,000. At the same time, Madero had sufficiently consolidated his position in the Mexican capital to pay some attention to the filibusters on the Baja Peninsula.

With the help of the powerful General Harrison Otis, Madero reached an agreement with President Taft under which

81

Mexican troops could be transported to Baja California over United States territory. The troops were to be unarmed while in the United States, but the agreement stated that arms could be carried in baggage cars. When word of this reached Colonel Vega in Enseñada, he no longer remained aloof to the problem in Mexicali and Tijuana. He organized an army of almost 600 and marched on Tijuana. Moseby sobered up his Wobblies and outlaws and went out on a train to meet the Vega forces. Moseby was outnumbered almost six to one and his army of wenching faro players was no match for the Vega forces. Several of his men were killed after a brief fight a few miles south of Tijuana. Those who survived fled back to the United States and were promptly arrested as they crossed the border. At the same time, in Mexicali, a group of Mexican vigilantes quickly rounded up the remnants of Moseby's forces in that city. Some were killed; the rest pushed back across the United States border where they, too, were delivered to the United States Army. The last filibuster in Mexico was ended. It was ended before the arrival of the federal troops from Mexico.

There was a Congressional hearing over the invasion, but, as is generally the case, little came of it. Flores Magon, who never did return to Mexico alive was jailed for violation of the United States neutrality laws. After completing his sentence at McNeil Island in Washington, he later was convicted of an espionage charge and sentenced to Leavenworth, where he died on November 21, 1922. In 1945, his body was taken to Mexico City where his remains were interred in the Rotunda of Illustrious Men. He is a subject of controversy in Baja, but throughout most of the rest of Mexico, his reputation is assured.

Moseby, after his return to the United States, was arrested for desertion from the United States Marine Corps. After conviction of the charge, he was sentenced to jail and en route was shot and killed while attempting to escape. Pryce is believed to have died in San Francisco's skid row.

Immediately after Moseby's defeat, Ferris the Bold went back to the stage with his wife, where he played to packed houses as the lead man in a production named *Man From Mexico*. He became interested in aviation and promoted several air races successfully. In 1921, he formed the Yellow Cab Company in Los Angeles and from then on lived quietly until his death in 1933.

To his death, he was convinced that he was the man responsible for keeping the revolution going as long as it did. "That was a lost cause before it started," he once confided to a friend. "They all would have been run out of Mexico within twenty-four hours if I hadn't showed them how to keep it going."

Ricardo Castillo, a prominent Tijuana restaurateur and historian, disagrees. "Magon was a hero to many Mexicans," he says. "At the time, the whole nation was lost and there were many loyalties. Many believed in Magon as deeply as others believed in Madero or Diaz. It was the interference from this press agent, Ferris, that kept the Mexican supporters away from Magon. Without that, Bajans possibly would have rallied behind the so-called Magon Army and have gained control of the entire Baja Peninsula as well as Sonora. Ferris was a man of pure brass. It is quite possible that he may have lost Magon the war."

There is a strange sidelight to the antics of Ferris the Bold and his press agentry in Baja California. The banquet room in which he held his dinner party to celebrate his "election" as provisional president of the newly formed Republic of Madero was never used again.

At one time, the Alexandria Hotel was among the most popular in Los Angeles and its suites have been occupied by Presidents Taft, Wilson, and Theodore Roosevelt, along with many of the world's famous personalities. Because of Ferris the Bold, however, it became half the hotel it once was.

Today, no one knows who made the reservation for the banquet room where the Ferris celebration dinner was held.

83

Thus, no one knows who was responsible financially for puncturing an oil painting that was hanging in the room. The painting was on loan from a local artist, uninsured, and the price that the owner placed on the damage to his work was termed exorbitant by one partner in the hotel, a Mr. Kreedman, and reasonable by the other, a Mr. Roddee.

The disagreement triggered a lifelong feud between the two partners. Roddee wrote out a check to pay for the painting from hotel funds and then gave the artist his work to take back to his studio to repair. When Kreedman brought up the matter to Roddee, he suggested that since the hotel had paid such an exorbitant price for the painting, it was the property of the hotel and therefore should be returned to the hotel as soon as possible and remain permanently in its possession. Roddee demurred. The painter was a close friend of Mrs. Roddee's and the check had been paid to cover the damage to the painting, not for the painting itself. Unfortunately for the painter, who had two other works on display in the same room, the argument became very heated and unresolved. Eventually Roddee stormed out of the hotel and went to his home, leaving his partner Kreedman brooding in his office.

A short time later, Kreedman came up with a possible solution to the dilemma. He could not remove the paintings and take possession of them because that would be theft. There was, however, nothing to prevent them from being shown publicly. Subsequently, before he left the hotel, he ordered his maintenance department to put a new lock on the door to the room and give him all of the keys to it.

The following day, Roddee learned of his partner's behavior and understandably was upset. Again, there was a heated argument with Kreedman. Before this one was over the two men had decided to dissolve their partnership. Neither of the partners wished to buy the other out, however, as both wished to remain in the hotel business. A compromise was reached. The hotel would be divided into two equal parts and a toss of the coin would determine who would build the new entrance. Roddee lost the toss. Kreedman kept the name of the Alexandria and the existing lobby.

The very next morning, work was started on the division of the hostelry. The corridors on each of the eight floors were sealed off by brick walls. The partnership was legally dissolved. At the same time, Roddee started work on a new lobby and a new entrance to the portion he had retained. Construction had gone on for several weeks before Roddee made a terrible discovery. There were neither stairs nor an elevator leading up from the first floor of his half of the building, nor was there any practical way that a stairwell or elevator shaft could be installed. Even a fire escape could not be installed unless it descended the face of the hotel and marred its appearance. Roddee took down his awnings, boarded up the entrance, and went home to figure out an answer to his problem. He never did.

Up through World War II, the Alexandria remained one of the more popular spots in the city. Its dining room was considered one of the best. Name bands played nightly in its ballroom, but few, if any, of the patrons realized that it was only half the hotel it used to be. Both Kreedman and Roddee had passed on. The Alexandria still exists, patronized during the day by lawyers and bankers who have their offices nearby. At night, its patrons are basically businessmen from out of town who wish an address convenient to the offices of the banks and attorneys.

Until 1967, the sealed-off portion of the hotel remained intact, with more than 130 rooms still furnished and still inaccessible. A passerby, if he had the inclination, could still peek through the boards to the partially finished lobby that never saw a guest. Until this year, Miss Lee Roddee, then seventy, still paid the taxes and insurance on the building, but then, after a tax hike, she decided to have it razed to make room for a parking lot.

The banquet room where Ferris the Bold had made his presidential acceptance speech was in the Roddee portion of the hotel. When the wreckers started their work, the daughter of the artist whose painting had been punctured more than a half-century earlier, Mrs. Roberta Ullman, was present. Workmen helped her up a ladder to the second floor, where the room was located, and broke down the still-locked door. The dust was three quarters of an inch thick. No one possibly could have been in the room for years.

There were no paintings on the wall.

A COUPLE OF LOST SQUADRONS

The United States Navy has always prided itself on the caliber of its officers, with particular reference to their ability to follow orders. A good example of this discipline can be found to this day upon a rocky section of the Pacific Coast some twenty-five miles north of Santa Barbara. On the evening of September 9, 1923, a squadron of seven destroyers was heading south a few miles off the shore. The weather was a little foggy, but the flotilla was proceeding in close formation and at full speed. The captain of the lead destroyer absentmindedly made a left-hand turn and the whole flotilla sailed at full speed into the rocky shore. The destroyers were upended like plastic boats in a bathtub, but

87

miraculously, although the injured list was long, only twenty-two sailors were drowned.

The committees investigating the disaster could understand how one commanding officer, a skipper, could inadvertently run his ship at full steam into the shore, but they found it odd that the six other skippers would blindly follow him to destruction, until someone explained that in the Navy, officers were taught to follow orders and that this was a prime example of disciplinary responsibility.

In view of this prime example of the Navy's sense of duty and discipline, it is rather difficult to explain how the Navy ever came to commission one Thomas Ap Catesby Jones as a commodore some three quarters of a century earlier. Possibly it was because of Jones that the Navy no longer boasts the rank of commodore. In the historical annals of the United States Navy, the adventures of Commodore Jones are conveniently overlooked and one can easily understand why, if he understands the Navy's sensitivity toward discipline.

Jones came from a proper New England family and was appointed to the Naval Academy, where he was graduated without an indication that he might be inclined to erratic behavior. It took him fifteen years to rise in rank from ensign to commodore, which was about average, and he had to wait an additional two years before he was given a command of his own.

On December 4, 1841, the Secretary of the Navy, Abel Upshur, announced that because of the unsettled conditions in the Northern Hemisphere, he was increasing the size of the United States naval force in the Pacific Ocean by one squadron. The squadron consisted of six ships and was placed under the command of Commodore Thomas Ap Catesby Jones. The commodore took his fleet on a leisurely voyage around the Horn and eventually reached the California coast. California at this time was owned by Mexico.

For several weeks, the fleet tarried in San Diego as guests of the Mexican government, then slowly proceeded up the coast, eventually reaching the Mexican capital of California at Monterey. At this time, the United States was at peace with Mexico, but as Jones said several years later, he had no way of knowing this because communications were extraordinarily poor between the fleet in the Pacific and the Navy headquarters in Washington. As a result, on a warm spring day in 1842, Commodore Jones sailed his fleet into the harbor of Monterey and proceeded to capture it. The capture was not a difficult feat. His warships lobbed a few cannonballs into the hills in back of the town. He sent a landing party ashore to arrest Governor Micheltorena and a few other assorted government officials. He then granted liberty to most of his men to celebrate the occasion.

The citizens of the community did not seem particularly upset over this turn of events, but the capture of a state capital of a friendly nation was not received in good favor by either the United States or Mexico when the news eventually reached these heads of government. The United States Secretary of State, Daniel Webster, personally apologized to the ambassador from Mexico in Washington. The American ambassador was ordered to convey his regrets to the government of Mexico in Mexico City. It took several days to get word to Commodore Jones that he was to turn Governor Micheltorena loose along with his assistants and to get his sailors out of Monterey and back on the ships.

Reluctantly, Commodore Jones complied, but he kept his squadron in the Monterey Harbor "in case hostilities did break out" and because there had been no orders issued for him to resume cruising. Once again, the Mexican government protested and once again the heads of state apologized to each other. Commodore Jones was to get out of Monterey Harbor and, additionally, he was to be relieved of his command as soon as

89

Commodore Dallas could arrive to take over. Jones was ordered to return to Washington "in such mode as be most convenient and agreeable" to himself. With typical military efficiency, the Navy also forgot to mention a spot where Jones could meet Dallas.

The phraseology of the orders apparently was the custom of the time in correspondence between officers and gentlemen, but it is unlikely that anyone in Washington had any idea as to how Commodore Jones would interpret his instructions. He found it most convenient and agreeable to sail with his fleet from Monterey to Hawaii, an area with which Washington found it even more difficult to maintain communications than Monterey.

Several months later, word was received in the nation's capital that its missing squadron was anchored off the shores of Honolulu. A few weeks after this, word was passed to Commodore Dallas as to where he could make his rendezvous. Dallas was sent across the Pacific in the frigate *Erie* to take over his command and to explain to Commodore Jones that a detour via Hawaii was not what the Navy had in mind when it told him to return in the "mode most convenient and agreeable to himself."

When Dallas arrived in Honolulu, however, he found no squadron and he learned from some other sailors and natives that the squadron had sailed a few weeks earlier for an unknown destination in the South Pacific. How long Dallas waited in Hawaii before he learned that the missing squadron of Commodore Jones was anchored in Tahiti is not on record.

Once again Dallas took off in pursuit only to discover, when he arrived in Papeete, that Commodore Jones again had set sail, with his next stop scheduled at Valparaiso in Chile. Weeks later, Dallas arrived in Valparaiso where he learned that Commodore Jones had sailed north the day after the first cold snap of winter had struck the city. Well aware of Commodore Jones's preference for a balmy tropical climate, Dallas immediately sailed

90

north, but still he could find no trace of the missing fleet. Dallas never did. He died in Callao, ironically, some three weeks before Commodore Jones sailed into the same port for refueling and reprovisioning.

It was here that the cruise of Commodore Jones took a more definite turn. Daniel Webster had secured orders from the Navy which were more explicit in ordering the wandering commodore to return to his base, and copies had been given to every consul-general or his representative at every port where Jones might put in for reprovisioning. In Callao, the consul-general boarded Jones's flagship almost before it dropped anchor and personally ordered Jones to go home immediately and in the most direct manner possible.

A good Navy man, Commodore Jones did not disobey his new orders. Once again he sailed south for the trip around the Horn. He paused at Valparaiso for supplies and while his ships were being provisioned, another U.S. Navy ship sailed into the bay. On board this ship was Commodore John Drake Sloat. He had been sent out to pick up the chase from the late Commodore Dallas and was overjoyed at running into the elusive Catesby Jones so early in the game.

Jones welcomed Sloat aboard and studied Sloat's orders carefully. He noted that although they had come from the Navy Department, they bore an earlier date than the instructions he had received in Callao and he presumed, therefore, they must be void. He refused to give up his command and, with the new commodore along as his guest, he sailed the squadron back to Washington, arriving there shortly after the inauguration of President James Knox Polk in 1845, more than three years after his departure.

The Navy Department apparently was most understanding. It agreed that there was some confusion over the orders that Sloat carried, but this was straightened out with a minimum of

91

difficulty. Commodore Sloat was put in command of the squadron after Jones was relieved of command and once again the flotilla was sent around the Horn to patrol the California coast.

No action ever was taken against Catesby Jones. Relations with Mexico at this time no longer were friendly and Commodore Jones was lauded by President Polk for his "elevated principles of duty." Neither Polk nor anyone else ever asked how the Navy could lose an entire squadron of ships for three years.

Catesby Jones was given a new assignment, but it was on shore. Never again was he given the opportunity to command a ship.

A few months after Commodore Sloat arrived in California, he sailed his squadron into Monterey Bay, lobbed a few cannonballs over the town into the hills, then sent a landing party ashore to take possession of the town. This time there was no problem. The United States was at war with Mexico.

A statue still stands in Monterey commemorating Commodore Sloat's capture of the city. There's not even a plaque to Catesby Jones.

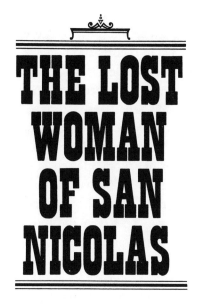

THE LOST WOMAN OF SAN NICOLAS

Lying some seventy-six miles out to sea from Los Angeles Harbor is the island of San Nicolas. Shaped somewhat like a prehistoric fish, it is approximately nine miles long and three and one half miles wide. For many centuries prior to the arrival of the Europeans, it was the home of an aboriginal tribe of Indians whose population fluctuated between five hundred and a thousand. They lived from the sea and from the birds and bore no similarities to the Indian tribes of the California coast.

San Nicolas also is the home of many hundreds of sea lions, seals, and walrus and for many thousands of birds such as ravens, cormorants, sea gulls, blue herons, canaries, larks, robins, and bald eagles. Like most of the other channel islands, San Nicolas has been bombarded with a continuing barrage by the United States Navy, but surprisingly, the birds and the pinnipeds have survived the assault. With one exception, however, the Indians showed no such tenacity to survive in their island home.

The Indians had lived on this small blot of an island for many hundreds of centuries before it was "discovered" in 1602 by the Spanish explorer Sebastian Vizcaino, who was searching for safe harbors where Manila treasure galleons could find shelter in case of trouble. He named the island La Isla de San Nicolas in honor of a patron saint of sailors. He sent a small boat ashore and was welcomed by Indians "living naked in the manner of savages and accustomed to public licentious practice." He marked it on the maps as a possible galleon haven and moved on.

For the next century and a half, San Nicolas went largely unnoticed and the Indian inhabitants remained in isolation. They had no boats, no nomadic inclinations, and they lived comfortably off the sea and bird life which abounded on the island. Before the island started to erode, anthropologists located some sixty-eight village sites and estimated the population had remained static at around one thousand persons.

In the early nineteenth century, San Nicolas was discovered to be a haven for otters and seals. Ships carrying hunters of these choice fur-bearing mammals descended upon the island with the regularity of a ferry boat. With this onslaught, the Indian population of San Nicolas began to decline. There are unconfirmed reports that some of the hunters killed the otters and the seals for profit and the Indians for sport. Many of the women were kidnapped and taken to Los Angeles for sport of a different nature. By 1835, the Indian population of San Nicolas had dwindled from an estimated thousand to slightly more than forty men and women.

It was at this time that some padres in a Franciscan mission decided that the remaining San Nicolas Indians would lead a happier life if they were brought to the mainland to work under the guidance of the good fathers. Accordingly, the padres chartered a schooner named *Peor Es Nada*, under the command of Captain Charles Hubbard, to sail out to San Nicolas and return to Los Angeles with the Indians. There are two versions as to how Captain Hubbard accomplished his assignment.

One story relates that Hubbard called all of the Indians together and explained to them that they would get much more to eat at the mission and find life much more enjoyable by avoiding the constant encounters with the seal and otter hunters. The Indians agreed that this was indeed true, and after gathering up their meager possessions, climbed on board the schooner. The supporters of this version have failed to explain how Hubbard was able to communicate with the Indians, who spoke a dialect unknown on the mainland.

The other version is less kind to the captain of the *Peor Es Nada*. It states that Hubbard drove the remaining Indians at musket point to the shore from where they were ferried by longboat to the waiting schooner. Those who would not come quietly were shot.

Both stories, however, concur in what happened next. A young Indian woman cried out that her child, or her baby brother, still was on the island and, as the schooner got underway, she leaped from its deck into the water and swam back to San Nicolas. Captain Hubbard did not bother to send a boat after her. He had a charter waiting to carry a group of otter hunters to Santa Rosa Island, and following this he was committed for another charter up the California coast to San Francisco.

The schooner was met at Los Angeles Harbor by Franciscan monks and before they set off for the San Gabriel Mission with their future Indian converts, Hubbard told them of the young Indian woman who had escaped. No one thought she could

95

live for long alone on the island and apparently no one thought it worth another seventy-six-mile voyage to capture her.

The last of the San Nicolas Indians soon were assimilated by the agrarian Indians working for the mission and after they had learned to speak Spanish, they reported that the young woman who had swum back to the island was the daughter of a chief who had been killed by the otter hunters and that it was true, indeed, that she had left behind a child whom she had hidden from Hubbard's raiders. By this time, several years had passed. Hubbard was dead. He had gone down with his schooner, which had floundered off the Golden Gate during a storm. The woman surely had not lived more than a few weeks and the island was left to the birds and the pinnipeds and the occasional forays of the otter hunters. The hunting expeditions now were few. There were so few otters left that trips to the outlying island were unprofitable.

On one of these rare expeditions, however, more than fifteen years later, two hunters named Thomas Jeffries and George Nidever, accompanied by some Indian helpers, spent two months on San Nicolas, shooting a cargo of seal and otter. Near the end of their expedition, on a warm summer night, one of the Indians in the party mentioned that he had seen a naked woman running across the ridge of a hill near where they were shooting the seals.

Nidever laughed and later back in Los Angeles he related the story as an example of how an Indian caught "squaw fever" after being separated from the opposite sex for a few weeks. His companion, Carl Detman, had heard the story of the missing daughter of the San Nicolas chief and of her escape from Hubbard and after telling Nidever of the legend, the two men became fascinated with the idea that the Indian might really have been a woman running across the ridge of the hill and that she could be the last of the San Nicolas tribe.

Three years later, in 1853, Nidever, accompanied by Detman, went back to San Nicolas on another otter hunting expedition, but this time they left the hunting to the Indians and undertook an exhaustive search of the island for some sign of the missing woman. It was Detman who found the first clue, some small footprints in soft earth near a fresh water spring.

The otter hunt was abandoned and the Indian hunters were pressed into the search. Three weeks later Detman found her. Accompanied by two Indians, he came up the eastern side of one of the peaks near the north end of the island. She was sitting in a camouflaged grass shelter, looking down on a beach where Nidever and another group of Indians were searching for her tracks. So well hidden was her lair that Detman would have passed it but for the low growl of a dog. When the woman saw Detman, she put her hand to the dog's neck to smooth his hackles, then slowly stood up and faced Detman with no expression on her face. From neck to knees she was encased in a dress made of green cormorant feathers and the sheen of the feathers was reflected in the sun. She showed no signs of fear.

Detman spoke to her softly and she replied in a language he could not understand. A moment later, when he motioned for her to come with him, she nodded slightly, then walked by his side down the hill where they joined the startled Nidever. A short time later, when she was invited by a gesture of the hands to step into the longboat that would take her to the anchored schooner, she did as she was asked. Her dog attempted to get in the boat, but she spoke to him softly and the animal went back to the beach and sat down on his haunches. When the schooner sailed for Santa Barbara the following morning, the dog was still on the beach.

Again there is a conflict in stories as to where she lived when she arrived in Santa Barbara. Some reports indicate she was placed in a convent near the Santa Barbara Mission where she was, in effect a ward of a Father Gonzales. A more accepted version is that she lived in the home of Nidever where his wife cared for her. No one could understand her, nor did she have the ability of other members of her tribe to learn even primary words in either English or Spanish. The monks at the Santa Barbara Mission attempted to locate one of the San Nicolas Indians who had been taken to San Gabriel, but all who had known her had either disappeared or died. A couple of second-generation members of her tribe were located, but they knew nothing of the native tongue of their parents.

The woman, who had been in perfect physical condition when she arrived in Santa Barbara, could not adjust to her new environment. Her cormorant dress, taken from her and replaced by "garments of a more decorous nature," was sent by the padres as a gift to the Pope and it presently can be seen in the Vatican Museum. She could not conform to a "proper diet." She was accustomed only to raw abalone and fish. She could not eat.

Within a month, she was too weak to walk. Within less than three months after her departure from San Nicolas, she died. Shortly before her death, she was baptized by a Santa Barbara priest who gave her the name of Juana Maria, and she was buried in the graveyard of the Santa Barbara Mission under that name. In 1928, the Santa Barbara Chapter of the Daughters of the American Revolution placed a plaque over her grave. The plaque refers to her only as an Indian woman who had been abandoned on San Nicolas for eighteen years.

The lost woman of San Nicolas was the last survivor of her tribe. For many years historians thought that the island was settled by Indians some six hundred years ago, but recent Carbon-14 tests of Indian artifacts on San Nicolas indicate that Indians lived there as far back as 2000 B.C. They left behind exquisitely carved creatures of the land, the sea, and the air, and they bear such a strong likeness to the artifacts of the Ghalas-at tribe of Alaska that there must be a relationship.

In the not too distant geological future, San Nicolas itself probably will become lost. After Nidever took home the last of its original inhabitants, sheep were introduced onto the island and within a few decades they had eaten the green to the sand and the rock. During World War II the Navy used it as a practice bombing range and then in 1946, the Navy turned it into a secret guided missile testing site. Today, the island has eroded into little more than a nine-mile stretch of lava rock and sand. The prevailing winds average between thirty-five and fifty miles per hour and often the sand is whipped into such a swirling mass that from a distance it appears as fog in the lee of the hills with waves gnawing at its feet. It is a mystery that the thousands of birds do exist in such a bleak and barren area. No longer could a young woman, or even a strong man, survive alone for eighteen years on San Nicolas.

San Nicolas will become lost, as did its inhabitants of some four thousand years ago.

LOST
ARTS

The art and petroglyphs of the lost San Nicolas Indians puzzle archaeologists no less than do the relatively recent discovery of intaglio art scraped into the floor of the Southwestern deserts of the United States and the common use of the amazing Minoan maze as a design by certain Indian craftsmen. There has been no reasonable answer advanced to explain the intaglios and the only possible answer to the riddle of the Minoan maze is that it was brought to the Southwest by descendants of the ancient Scythians.

In the fall of 1930, George Palmer, a Nevada airport operator, took off from Las Vegas to visit relatives who lived in a small community along the Colorado River near Blythe, California. After Palmer had crossed the Riverside Range and headed south, and while flying over the flat mesa country, he noticed a string of horse tracks spread out along the ground. A moment after this thought registered, he wondered how he could possibly see hoofprints from an altitude of more than 5000 feet. He looked again. The hoofmarks were still there. He shook his head. A horse that could leave tracks which could be seen from almost a mile in the sky would have to have hooves between three and four feet long and this, indeed, he thought would be one hell of a big horse. While he was speculating on this thought, he was even more astonished to see the outline of a crudely drawn man stretched on his back on top of a mesa. He banked and dropped down to about 2000 feet for a closer look. Not only was there the outline of a man, but next to it someone had delineated an extraordinarily immense horse and a coiled snake. The area was desolate. No one lived within miles and, he decided, it would be virtually impossible for anyone to scrape out a figure so huge without losing the proportions. Nevertheless, someone had.

When he landed at Blythe a short time later, he delayed the visit to his relatives and called upon some pioneer residents of the community to ask about the strange figures. Many of them had traveled the area on prospecting trips, but none could recall seeing any such figures. He was looked upon in much the same manner as a man who has just seen a flying saucer.

Upon his return to Las Vegas, Palmer made it a point to fly over the area once again, convinced that he had suffered some form of temporary aberration and that the figures would be non-existent. They were still there. He flew over them for about a half hour, carefully marking their location on his air map. When he returned to Las Vegas, he made a crude sketch of his discovery, wrote a detailed report of what he had seen and sent it and the air map to the Southwest Museum in Los Angeles.

The Museum made a record of the contribution, but be-

101

cause there were no roads going into the area and because it was the start of the Depression and no money was available to finance an investigation of the discovery, the matter rested in the files until 1952.

During World War II, the intaglios were once again "discovered," this time by military pilots on air maneuvers over the desert. It was on the basis of these reports, plus the Palmer sightings, that the National Geographic Society and the Smithsonian Institution sent archaeologists into the field who not only confirmed the Palmer sightings, but found additional intaglios on the opposite side of the Colorado River, in Arizona.

The largest of the Blythe figures was a woman 171 feet long with outflung arms spanning a distance of 158 feet. There were three other figures in this group. One was a male measuring 95 feet, and the other consisted of an animal and a coiled snake. The technique for making the intaglios had been rather simple. The artist, or artists, had merely removed a layer of desert-varnished rocks to expose the lighter colored earth beneath. Like the artifacts found on San Nicolas, the scientists estimated they were etched some time before the birth of Christ, which, incidentally, punches another hole in the oft-repeated story that the Spaniards introduced the horse to the New World.

Twelve years after the Blythe site had been explored, another set of giant effigies, also judged by experts to predate Christ, were discovered on a similar desert plateau in Peru. These intaglios were etched into yellow subsoil and outlined with dark stones. The Peruvian figures, located near Nazca, included a spider, a bird with an elongated beak, a killer whale, a 262-foot monkey and the the site's largest figure, a bird measuring 787 feet. Whether or not the Peru artists were related to those of the Colorado desert has never been determined.

A cluster of other giant intaglios then was discovered from the air in a remote area of Imperial County, California, adjacent to the Baja California border. Here the immense figures appear to represent matters of fertility, with huge phallic and womb symbols. Dr. Emma Lou Davis of the University of California at Los Angeles made a special study of them and estimated the age of these figures at 1500 years.

A peculiarity of all of these sites is that the figures are spread out on mesas over which there is no higher vantage point to observe the completed work. Because of their immense size, they are not recognizable from the ground and at the time they were made could be seen only by God and birds.

During the winter of 1966, some amateur archaeologists from Blythe discovered an ancient Indian village which Carbon-14 tests date back to approximately 8500 B.C. The village is in the same general area as the giant effigies discovered by Palmer. Ancient trails led to and from the village. When Dr. Davis surveyed the site, she determined that the trails were made by three different cultures. In many areas, the trails ran conspicuously parallel. No one has come up with a valid answer as to why later cultures refused to tread on a trail so firmly established that it still is clearly defined approximately 10,000 years after it first came into existence. Nor is there any speculation as to why the second trail was abandoned, in turn, by later inhabitants of the village. So rigid was the taboo against using the older trails that wherever they crossed, stone bridges were built to let the pedestrian pass safely.

Despite Palmer's report in 1930, it was not until 1967 that the huge horse tracks discovered by the pioneer aviator were studied scientifically from the ground. The exploration team was led by Dr. Davis, who found that the tracks closely approximated Palmer's calculations from the air. There are ten groups of prints, each shaped like a horseshoe with circular impressions measuring a little more than three feet across at the widest point. Flanking these ten prints are two straight rows of similar impressions and near each of these, are ten rock piles, a point which might indicate that these ancient and superstitious Indians preferred the decimal system. Indians who lived during the colonization era favored the numbers three, four, and seven, in both legend and religion.

On the same large plateau, and comparatively near the huge horse tracks, is a perfectly preserved dance circle, which also provides an element of mystery. On the arid Mojave desert, dance circles usually were small because, due to the dearth of food, desert Indians traveled and lived in small bands. When they danced, as is the custom today, they wanted to be somewhere within hailing distance of their fellow dancers. The mysterious dancing circle is immense. It would have taken hundreds upon hundreds of Indians to have created it.

It is a reasonable assumption that the giant horse prints, the dance circle, and the huge intaglios all spring from some cult that lived in the area eons ago and that all quite probably had a religious significance. Not so easily explained is the Minoan maze.

The Minoan maze is of circular design, so unique in appearance and intricate in structure that authorities on prehistoric rock art, such as Campbell Grant, have stated that it is a "million to one shot" that the symbol could have arisen independently in both the New World and the Old. At first glance, it looks like a partially melted heating unit from an electric stove, but it is a maze in the truest sense. To the superstitious, it could well be a symbol of bad luck because so many races that have used it have now become extinct. There is little mystery as to its antiquity.

Early representations of the Minoan maze are on coins struck more than 4,000 years ago in the Knossos Palace in Crete. Some sources contend that it symbolized the legend in which Ariadne gave her lover, Theseus, a spool of thread to guide himself out of the labyrinth he had entered to slay the Minotaur. The Minoan period, from which the maze gets its identity, dates from 2700 B.C. to 1100 B.C. when it came to an abrupt end because of a devastating earthquake. As far as is known, the Cretans had no written language. About a century before the earthquake, the Cretans were infiltrated by Scythians, who had been driven away by the Assyrians from their home in Eurasia. It is possible that the Scythians introduced the peculiar design into the Minoan culture, although most historians believe that the Scythians picked up the maze from the Cretans.

The Scythians moved on to the West and probably were responsible for introducing the distinctive maze into Etruscan art. An excellent example was found on an Etruscan vase dated about 700 B.C. Although the Etruscans could write, no scholar has been able to decipher their language, so if any ancient Etruscan ever bothered to chronicle the origin of this peculiar symbol, there is no one around who can read it.

It is known that the Scythian tribes migrated slowly to the north, and examples of the Minoan maze have been found etched in glacial rocks in the Camonica Valley of the Italian Alps. The Scythians then continued north to that part of England now known as Wales and generally are considered to be the forebears of the Welsh. Others moved on to Ireland, recording their presence by engraving still another Minoan maze into a massive block of granite in the Irish Wicklow Mountains where, for some unknown reason, it now is referred to as "The Hollywood Stone." Across the St. George Channel from Wicklow, on a ledge in Rocky Valley in Cornwall, England, are engraved two other Minoan mazes.

It was not until recently that scholars realized the Minoan maze had made the long leap to the New World many hundreds of years ago and thus provided a clue to one of the great mysteries of the Southwest: the identity of a lost civilization that was in existence before the fall of Babylon.

This civilization is referred to today as the Hohokam, which literally means nothing, as it is a word taken from the

105

Pima tribes meaning the "unknown ones." At the peak of their period, their culture embraced more than two hundred and fifty cities with a capital in what is now known as Casa Grande. The date it was founded is unknown to archaeologists. An agrarian race, they developed a highly complicated and efficient irrigation system which ran off the Gila, the Salt, and the Santa Cruz rivers. One canal was more than a half-mile wide and extended for more than seventeen miles.

So well engineered were their canals that in many areas, they had devised a system whereby the water ran uphill, a feat which most historians believe was first devised by the ancient Minoans. Like the Minoans also, the Hohokams were fond of leisure and sports. They built special floors and marked them in the manner of a modern tennis court and near one, the remnants of a rubber ball have been found encased in caliche.

The New York of the nation was a large city, its name unknown, but whose ruins were named by the Spaniards as Casa Grande, or "large house." The area now is a national park.

Etched into a second-floor wall of this prehistoric palace is a huge Minoan maze. It has long been recognized as such by scholars and one explanation that was accepted until recently is that the design was carved on the wall by a passing Spanish soldier. This theory was discarded, however, when archaeologists determined that the second floor of the ancient palace collapsed some years before Columbus set sail on his voyage of discovery and the only way any Spaniard could have etched the design was for him to have built a complicated scaffolding system that would enable him to get that high above the floor.

Then another Minoan maze design was found carved into a wall near Oraibi in northeastern Arizona and shortly after this discovery, four more were found in the same area. Scholars found another in a nearby Hopi Indian village and then still another in the Galisteo Basin in New Mexico.

Diggers then began to unearth pottery shards with portions of the Minoan maze inscribed upon them when another discovery was made belatedly. Pima Indians, who live in the area, many of whom are fair-skinned and blue-eyed, still were using the design in pottery they were making. When asked if there was any significance to this choice of design, they replied with a shrug and indicated that it had been passed down for years.

The archaeologists have been able to determine that the mysterious Hohokams were in the area about 300 B.C. and apparently reached the peak of their empire around 1300 when, like the Mayans far to the south, most of them suddenly vanished. Why they abandoned their cities is unknown.

The ruins of many Hohokam cities still can be found around Arizona, but the most accessible probably are the Casa Grande north of Tucson and the Pueblo Grande near Phoenix.

There is a legend that the Romans lost an expedition near Tucson and that the Phoenicians once sailed up the Rio Puerco in New Mexico, as related by these writers in *The Mysterious West*. There is a strong possibility that the Scythians moved on from Wales to Arizona. How else can one explain the irrigation expertise and the appearance of the ubiquitous Minoan maze?

107

A FEW LOST LADIES

Other than in a few religious circles, there has always been a fondness for the lost ladies who have strolled the primrose path in the West. They never were referred to contemptuously as prostitutes, but rather by their names, which ranged from French Rosarita to Tugboat Annie. Prostitution still is legal in the State of Nevada, except in Clark County where it has been banned at the request of casino operators who want nothing to distract the attendance from the gaming tables. (The law here requires that even the swimming pools in the hotels must close down at 6 P.M. in order to get the sunbathers back to the crap tables.) Houses still operate in most of the Northwestern states in a semi-legal manner, except for Oregon, where an attorney-general named Robert Y. Thornton closed them down in the mid-fifties, apparently as a concession to the Methodist vote. They started closing in California somewhat earlier, except for one holdout in Jackson in the center of the state in what is known as the Mother Lode Country. This town was not forced to turn its girls out into the street until 1956, when California Attorney-General Edmund G. (Pat) Brown followed the Thornton syndrome.

Brown did not have an easy time carrying out his crusade in Jackson. Sid Smith, one of the Mother Lode's better-known chroniclers, recalls that Brown first sent plainclothesmen from his office into Jackson in 1951 to check on reports that bordellos were operating openly.

"They didn't have much trouble in finding the action," Smith recalls. "They asked directions from a local cop. Brown then complained to the chief-of-police, who shut them down. The next day, the city council fired the chief and replaced him with a new one, so the houses only lost one day of business."

Complaints from Brown to the new chief evoked a reply that he had "looked around and couldn't find anything like that going on."

In the spring of 1956, Brown sent in some state officers who dropped into the four operating houses and arrested approximately fifty persons. This effectively shut down a local industry that had been operating in the community for more than a century, when the town first became an entity known as Botilleas because of the empty whiskey bottles abandoned by miners.

About a decade later, a group of Jackson businessmen were discussing the numerous plaques that had been erected around the Mother Lode Country as historical markers for the edification of passing tourists. One of them lamented the fact that no recognition ever had been given to the last of the California whorehouses in Jackson. It was an oversight that the group decided to rectify.

109

Immediately they banded into a committee known as the Environmental Resources Enabling Committee to Investigate Our Necessary Services, with its objective to place a bronze historical marker in front of the old bordellos.

The mayor thought the idea an excellent one, as did the chief of police. The plaque was cast, encased in cement and unveiled a few weeks later before television cameras brought from as far as Los Angeles and San Francisco. The plaque was built in the shape of a heart. In the upper left-hand section was a red lantern and balancing it on the right was a dollar sign. The inscription read:

BOTILLEAS BORDELLOS

———

WORLD'S OLDEST PROFESSION
FLOURISHED 50 YDS. EAST OF
THIS PLAQUE FOR MANY YEARS
UNTIL THIS MOST PERFECT
EXAMPLE OF FREE ENTERPRISE
WAS PADLOCKED BY
UNSYMPATHETIC
POLITICIANS

———

E.R.E.C.T.I.O.N.S.

The plaque was installed on a Valentine's Day. The attack on the commemorative plaque was started the following Sunday by Reverend Wayne Long of Jackson's Methodist Church, who charged the installation was a crack in the door to bring back prostitution. This was followed by a plethora of anonymous calls from elderly ladies demanding that the offending plaque be removed. The city council refused. Wax casts were made of the inscription and smaller replicas appeared in the bars around Jackson. Reverend Long increased the tempo of his crusade and the number of anonymous telephone calls from indignant ladies increased. Three or four days later, someone dumped a bucket of red paint over the inscription. Sometime during the dark hours of the sixth day following the unveiling, someone dug the plaque from the cement. No one knows where it was taken. The anonymous telephone calls dwindled and then ceased.

"It was the women," says Smith. "Most of them are pretty unreasonable when it comes to whoring. Why, when Julia Bullette was buried, there wasn't one woman who attended her funeral just because she ran a pleasure palace, yet if it hadn't been for Julie, the North might have lost the Civil War."

Julia Bullette was a dark-eyed, black-haired beauty of unknown origin. There are some reports which say she came to Virginia City, Nevada, directly from London. Others report she was a Creole who followed Horace Greeley's advice when she became tired of working in the French Quarter of New Orleans. No one in Nevada particularly cared. The women hated her and all men but one loved her, not only in a professional sense, but for what she did for Virginia City.

If an epidemic swept through the city, Julia closed the doors to her palace at the corner of Union and D streets and spent days helping the sick. She was one of the town's heaviest contributors to the Sanitation Fund, a forerunner of the Red Cross and, upon one occasion, when the community was attacked by Paiutes, Julia was the only woman who refused to seek safety, preferring instead to stay with the men and bandage their wounds. She was the only woman ever to be elected an honorary member of Virginia City Engine Company Number One. Whenever there was a parade, she rode on the engine and whenever her company answered a fire call, Julia Bullette was on hand with coffee and refreshments for the firefighters.

Her palace was a gourmet's delight. Before anyone reached

a satin-covered bed, he was engaged in "good conversation," and offered skillfully prepared French dishes and the finest wines and champagne. It can be presumed that the fee for a dalliance with Julia was far more costly than in some other houses of pleasure around Virginia City. One of the Comstock Mines was named the "Julia" in her honor and the best club car of the Virginia and Truckee Railroad bore the gold-plated name "Julia Bullette." When newly elected Governor Nye came to Virginia City, it was Julia who entertained him and other state functionaries at dinner, while the "good women" of the town gnashed their teeth behind closed curtains.

She ran her own poverty program, available for almost any legitimate touch; yet she retained enough to earn the reputation of being the best-dressed woman between San Francisco and Chicago. On most of her appearances in public, she was accompanied by her favorite lover, Tom Peasley, who incidentally also was chief of Engine Company Number One. At the Opera House, she kept her own loge and during summer productions she would be seen wearing an opera hood of white silk and the latest fashionable dress. In the winter, she often appeared wearing her prized sable cape and muff.

In Virginia City, as in other towns of the West, a killing was not uncommon. Most attracted no more than a passing comment, but when Julia Bullette was found murdered, every male but one was shocked.

Her body was found on the morning of January 20, 1867, a Sunday, by a friendly competitor named Gertrude Holmes, who had entered Julia's palace through the back door to share breakfast. After receiving no answer to her call, Gertrude discreetly tiptoed up the stairs to see if Julia was engaged with a client of means, left over from the preceding night. She was lying naked on the bed. Her clothes, in an untidy pile, were on the floor and it was obvious to Gertrude that Julia had died suddenly and not from natural causes. Her legs were partially over the edge of the bed, as if in the last seconds of life, she had started to get up, before being struck over the head with a club.

Two doctors were called and both agreed that Julia had been dead for approximately eight hours, that she had been hit over the head by a heavy stick, which was found in the room, and that she had been strangled while unconscious. The outraged males of Virginia City scoured the town looking for a satisfactory suspect to lynch, but none could be found. Early in the afternoon, one hapless visitor from San Francisco was collared, but he escaped the noose when he was able to prove that he had spent the night with one of Gertrude's girls.

By evening, the city was in mourning. Most of the men, from mayor to miner, spent the night outside the funeral home containing Julia's coffin. The only evidence that had been gathered was the statement of a newsboy who had heard a scream about five in the morning. The motive apparently had been robbery, for Tom Peasley could not find many pieces of Julia's jewelry. The following day, every business in Virginia City from casino to haberdashery was shut down. The Olympic Road Company canceled its appearance at the Opera House, but none of the cast dared leave the city for fear that suspicion might be directed toward one of them.

The funeral for Julia Bullette took place on Tuesday and it was the grandest ever to be held in the city. Her body was placed in a special silver-handled coffin which was borne in a black-plumed, glass-walled hearse. It was preceded in the procession to the graveyard by an eighteen-piece band and the marching men of the Virginia City Engine Company Number One. It was followed by more than two thousand mourners, all men. The wives, who would have no part in the services, pointedly drew their shades, or shuttered their windows, as the cortège passed. On the way to the cemetery, the band played funeral dirges, but on its return it turned to more festive tunes, such as "The Girl I Left Behind Me" and "When the Saints Come Marching In."

Approximately three months after the murder, the sheriff arrested one of the most avid mourners and charged him with killing Julia Bullette. His name was John Millain. He was recognized first by Martha Camp, another prominent madam, as a man she had surprised in her room a few nights earlier. He had made an attempt to stab her with a knife, but had fled when her screams attracted some of her clients. While he was being held in jail, a Gold Hill matron indignantly reported that Millain had sold her a dress pattern which originally had been sold "to that Bullette woman." Then the sheriff found that Millain had sold some of Julia's diamonds to a local jeweler and then, it was discovered, a trunk which Millain had left with a friend contained most of Julia's furs, including her sable cape, a large amount of her clothes, her jewelry, and a few silver bricks with her name engraved upon them.

The men of Virginia City wanted a quick trial and a hanging. The good women were opposed. They not only doubted the guilt of such a charming Frenchman, but argued that even if he were guilty, he had only rid the community of a harlot. They came in droves to Millain's cell, bringing him wines, hand-knit sweaters and socks and pâté de foie gras that had been brought overland from San Francisco. They circulated petitions, one calling for his immediate release and another, after he was convicted, demanding that his sentence be commuted to life imprisonment.

The trial was not a long one. There was no need for it to be, as the jury was all male and wanted to get on with the hanging.

The trial lasted one day. In his summation, District Attorney Bishop said: "Although this community has, in times past, seen blood run like water, in most cases there has been some cause brought forward in justification of the deed, some pretext.

114

The skull found in Calavaras County, California, in 1866 and pronounced by some experts to be more than a million years old. *Peabody Museum, Harvard University*

Francisco "Pancho" Villa with his wife. Between them is Ramon Contreras, one of Pancho's bodyguards. *Westways Magazine*

The remains of the mass murderer Quejo. The half-Cocopah Indian did away with more than twice as many victims as Billy the Kid.

he Arizona Territorial Prison at Yuma.
estways Magazine

Captain F. S. Ingalls, superintendent of the Arizona Territorial Prison.
Westways Magazine

The cell blocks were primitive in the Arizona Territorial Prison at Yuma. The few prisoners who were able to escape were captured by Indians and returned for a fifty-

This grave supposedly marks the site where W. D. Salmon, one of the victims of the mysterious Wickenburg Massacre, was buried. No one today is sure where the ambush occurred.
Dana Purden

Jack Mosby (left), the "soldier" most often elected general by the filibusterers when they held Tijuana.
Historical collection, Title Insurance and Trust Company, San Diego, California

Sand bags, placed around the Customs House at Tijuana during the invasion taken over by Ferris the Bold, were used to create an illusion of a military zone for North American

Invasion to enter the city.

Historical collection, Title Insurance and Trust

Sentries, such as this, were rare. The soldiers that invaded Tijuana were not the best disciplined troops. *Historical collection, Title Insurance and Trust Company, San Diego, California*

When a Mexican Army eventually marched from Ensenada against the filibusterers holding Tijuana, the invaders were rounded up from the bars, put on a commandeered train, and sent out to meet the Federalists.

The filibusterers at San Ysidro, where they were taken into custody by United States troops.

The smashup of seven U.S. Navy destroyers on the California coast five miles north of Santa Barbara on September 9, 1923. *Los Angeles Times*

Ruins of the Casa Grande in Arizona.
National Park Service

A view of the mysterious Minoan Maze carved on a high wall of the Casa Grand
National Park Service

Julia Bullette; this portrait hangs in
Virginia City's Bucket of Blood Saloon.
Golden West

The grave of Julia Bullette with Virginia City in the background.

The cornerstone of the old Presbyterian mission long abandoned in the New Mexico ghost town of Trementina.
Woodfin Camp

The towers from which Charles Hatfield the rainmaker sent his magic potions pouring into the sky, and brought down the waters in San Diego, California.
Historical collection, Title Insurance and Trust Company, San Diego, Californi

ne of the first dams to collapse, as a result of Hatfield the rainmaker, was the
veetwater Dam.

Another bridge washed out through the powers of Hatfield the rainmaker in the older section of the City of San Diego.

Charles Hatfield looks over newspaper accounts of his powers. The city never paid him.
Historical collection, Title Insurance and Trust Company, San Diego, Californ

reasures ranging from Spanish gold to Confederate money have been found in e rugged lava flow from Mount Taylor in central New Mexico.
. L. James

.iis baby sea serpent was caught by Al Dixon off Newport Beach, California. .other one about ten times as long got away.
T. Peabody, courtesy of Westways Magazine

This prehistoric minnow was caught by a fisherman in Lake Mojave.

This rare photo of a "Big Foot" was taken by Roger Patterson of Yakima, Wa ington. Patterson, who has been trailing the elusive creatures for more tha decade, managed to get within camera range in a remote northern Califo valley. Anthropologists have labeled the tracks left by the Big Foot as "mysteri and "authentic."

However, on the morning of the twentieth of January last, this community, so hardened by previous deeds of blood, was struck dumb with horror by a deed which carried dread to the heart of everyone . . . a deed more fiendish, more horrible than ever perpetrated on this side of the snowy Sierra. Julia Bullette was found lying dead in her bed, foully murdered, and stiff and cold in her clotted gore. True, she was a woman of easy virtue. Yet hundreds in this city have had cause to bless her name for her many acts of charity . . . and the nation, indeed, is indebted. But for her, the Union might not have been preserved."

The hanging of John Millain attracted even more people than the funeral of Julia Bullette. Virginia City took on a festive air. The gallows were erected in a natural amphitheater about a mile from the city, where at least five thousand persons could see the execution. Unlike Julia's funeral, which attracted only males, this audience brought out the good women of Virginia City, who wept as they scolded their happy husbands. Millain's last statement was to thank the good ladies of Virginia City for their concern over his welfare and for the delicacies they had brought to him in prison.

According to legend in Virginia City, every married man in the community, except for the preachers, spent the night of the hanging away from his connubial bed, and the girls in the palaces of pleasure were so exhausted by daylight that all of the bordellos were closed down for three days.

Another legend that still persists is that without Julia's help, the North might have lost the Civil War. This is based upon the fact that most of the miners who worked the rich silver mines were from the South and their sympathies naturally were with the Confederacy. The mine operators, the politicians, and the hierarchy of Virginia City were sympathetic to the Union. According to the legend, at one time during the war, when the Union was in desperate need of money, an incredibly large shipment of silver bricks to New York from the fabulously rich Comstock Lode was scheduled to go out by wagon train from Virginia City.

From a miner, Julia learned that the entire shipment was to be hijacked and diverted to the South. Julia put on her finest silks and rode out of Virginia City with the wagon train. The diversion was avoided because not a miner placed his sympathy for the South above his love for Julia.

Julia's sympathies obviously were with the North. She was a black.

A COUPLE OF LOST TOWNS

Most of the ghost towns of the West tell the same tale. They came into being because of a mine and when the mine was played out, so did the town play out, except for a few hangers-on who were charter members of the community's booster committee. Such towns are all over the West, but few have much history worth relating.

An exception, perhaps, is the California ghost town of Columbia, in the Mother Lode Country not far from Jackson, where the plaque dedicated to the oldest example of free enterprise raised such a furor.

Columbia was one of the latest cities to come into being

117

during the California gold rush, and it was born because of some loose talk by a group of Mexican prospectors. Some three or four members of the Mexican group let it drop in Botilleas one night that they had found a rich one. As a result, they were followed back to their claim by a group of American prospectors headed by a Thaddeus Hildreth. The Hildreth party ran off the Mexicans when the yield was discovered to be between fifteen and twenty pounds of gold daily. Imaginatively, they named their claim Hildreth's Diggings.

A few days later, some of Hildreth's party drifted back to Botilleas and after a few drinks made the same mistake as the Mexicans. Within three months the population of the area had grown to five thousand and the name of the town was changed to American Camp. Within three years, the population was up to some thirty thousand, the name of the town had been changed to Columbia, and it had a chamber of commerce and a daily newspaper, *The Star*.

By 1853, it was the second largest city in California and some members of the Columbia Boosters Club decided that the town should become the state capital of California. The capital at that time was located in Benecia, a coastal community a few miles north of San Francisco. Had it not been for the activities of a resourceful young attorney named Horace Bull, Columbia quite probably would not have lost its bid to become the seat of the state capital.

The Columbia Boosters Club drew up a petition for the state legislature which was signed by more than ten thousand of the local citizens, requesting that the capital be moved to Columbia. While awaiting the appointment of a committee to carry the petition to Benecia, the document was placed in a Columbia bank vault for safekeeping.

While the petition was in circulation, there had been an incident in one of Columbia's saloons over the favors of one of

118

the barmaids. As a result, a gentleman named Peter Nichols of Saw Mill Flat fatally stabbed one John Peroit of Pine Log. Because of the Booster Club influence, an instant trial and subsequent hanging were not in vogue in Columbia, so the bar patrons merely took Nichols down to the jail and turned him over to the sheriff. Nichols was allowed to hire an attorney, Horace Bull, and the case did not go to trial until six days after the murder.

Despite the efforts of Mr. Bull, Nichols was found guilty and sentenced to be hanged. Mr. Bull promptly served notice that he would appeal. Approval for this was granted, provided he got the whole matter straightened out within ten days in order that the hanging could be carried out. Mr. Bull appealed the case in a most unorthodox manner.

He went to the Boosters Club and explained that inasmuch as he had to go to Benecia to file his appeal, he would be glad to take along the petition. The Boosters Club thought this to be a practical suggestion and turned the petition over to Bull. The attorney then scissored off the portion of the petition pertaining to the proposed shift in the state capital and pasted over the ten thousand signatures a request for Governor John Bigler to spare the life of, and grant a pardon to, Peter Nichols.

When the governor saw the petition and realized the popularity of the defendant, he commuted the sentence immediately. Bull had successfully appealed the case and Columbia had lost its bid to become the state capital.

Understandably, Nichols disappeared as soon as his pardon came through and eventually the Columbia Boosters Club discovered Bull's perfidy. The resourceful Bull, however, offered to make up for his delinquency by giving the town a new fire engine, an offer which was accepted. In fact, he promised the city the finest fire engine in California and with a delivery date of about two weeks.

Waiting on the San Francisco docks was a new fire engine

119

built for King Kamehameha III of Hawaii. The Hawaiian monarch never received his fire engine. No one apparently knows just how it was done, but the fire engine was delivered in Columbia by Bull within a week. In appreciation for his donation, Bull was elected chief of the Columbia Fire Company Number One.

There is another ghost town in the Southwest: Trementina, New Mexico, that may hold the secret to the whereabouts of the long lost mine of Father La Rue in Los Organos Mountains.

Father La Rue was the adopted name of the son of a rich French farmer. According to legend, he joined a monastery when his father refused him permission to marry his sweetheart because of an insufficient dowry. When his studies were finished, he was sent to Mexico and assigned to clerical duties in a small village north of Durango. For a few years he taught and converted the Indians to Catholicism and tended to the wants of soldiers traveling between New Mexico and Mexico City.

Father La Rue was not a man of mercy. One version of his learning of the rich gold mine in Los Organos contends that he rifled the bags of an aging soldier who was spending the night in the village and that, after discovering a map which would guide him to the mine site, he dispatched the soldier with a quick thrust of a dirk. Another version says that the soldier told the priest of the mine shortly before he died.

It is known that Father La Rue suddenly decided that life in a village north of Durango was rather dull. He picked up several members of his flock and took off for Los Organos, where he did find the mine near what is now St. Augustine Pass on Soledad Canyon between Espiritu Santo Springs and La Cueva de las Vegas, overlooking the Mesilla Valley.

He built a small fortified village around the colony and not only proceeded to mine the rich ore, but built an underground smelter which refined the ore into gold bricks. Whenever an

Indian chanced by the site he was either sent on his way or killed by colony guards.

Supplies were brought in from Mesilla and paid for with gold dust, which was the preferred tender of the times.

After La Rue had been mining and smelting for a couple of years, the head of the diocese in Mexico City realized that it had been a long time, indeed, since they had heard from their station north of Durango. They assigned an investigator by the name of Maximiliano to look into the matter. The villagers reported only that the padre, accompanied by some fifty of his hand-picked parishioners, had gone north. Maximiliano trailed the party to Parral and learned from residents of this community that the missing priest had still been heading north when he passed through.

Several months later, the persistent Maximiliano had followed the trail as far as Mesilla. As first the merchants, aware of their good customer and wishing to keep him, reported that the party had traveled through, still headed north, but when Maximiliano could find no trace of them north of Mesilla, he returned to that community. By chance, he was present when Father La Rue's supply wagon came in for provisions. It wasn't much of a problem for such a persistent detective to trail the wagon back to the La Rue colony. Nor did it require much observation to determine what was going on.

Maximiliano confronted La Rue and demanded that all of the gold in the mine be turned over to Maximiliano as a custodian of the church, a proposal which Father La Rue regarded with disfavor on the grounds that the gold belonged to the colony and not to the church. Maximiliano left, promising to return with an army to seize it.

As soon as the investigator had departed, Father La Rue ordered all of the gold bricks placed in the mine and the shaft sealed. When Maximiliano returned a few weeks later with a

121

detachment of soldiers from Santa Fe, he was met with resistance. When the colony finally was overrun, nothing was found but a few stoic adults, including La Rue, who refused to show the stubborn detective or the soldiers the location of the shaft. After a few days of torture, an exasperated Maximiliano killed the priest in a fit of pique and eventually returned to Mexico City.

Shortly before the turn of the nineteenth century, a young man in Durango named Santiago Blea was married to Juanita Sanchez in the Catholic Church in Durango, Mexico. In appreciation for the ceremony, he presented the priest with a brick of gold weighing about ten pounds. Such a gift aroused the priest's curiosity. Blea was cooperative. He was descended from one of the men who had accompanied Father La Rue to the north, a man who had escaped and had left behind instructions as to how to reach the storeroom where the gold bricks were located. Santiago had been gone for several weeks and had come back with six of the bars, all that he could carry practically.

The priest explained to Santiago that the gold was the property of the church, a point which Santiago did not approve any more than had Father La Rue. His bride, however, insisted that the gold be turned over to the church. Whether or not Santiago succumbed to her wishes is not known.

According to the legend, however, both Santiago and Juanita fell into such disfavor with the priest that they left Durango. Years later, when Santiago died, Juanita used some of the gold to build a church "far north of Durango," in order to assuage any hard feelings that may have lingered over their use of the treasure which may have belonged to the Church. The legend says that the remaining gold bricks were buried at the site of the new church.

Some seventy miles to the north of Fort Sumner, New Mexico, is the mysterious ghost town of Trementina. The word means "turpentine" in Spanish and there are many piñon trees in

122

the area, which could have furnished a source for turpentine, although there are no signs of this industry in the ruins of the town. Unlike other ghost towns in the West, there is no indication of mining anywhere in the area. Shortly before the town was abandoned, it was chosen as the site for a Presbyterian mission, but this was never successful and it was closed down in the early 1930's. What makes the town worthy of mention, however, is the cornerstone for the Presbyterian mission, which was built at the start of the twentieth century. Chiseled into this large rock slab are words, in Spanish, which say, "Erected to the memory of Santiago Blea and Juana T. de Blea, 1912 s." Miss Alice Blake, the Presbyterian medical missionary who lived in the town, says the Presbyterian mission was built about 1912. There is no one around who can remember where the cornerstone was found or who has any idea why a Presbyterian church would use such a dedication stone. No one can recall anyone named Blea.

There is an intriguing aftermath to the legend of the La Rue Mine. In 1937, a Dr. Milton E. Noss, a chiropodist from Hot Springs, New Mexico, was deer hunting in the Los Organos Mountains when he stumbled upon a nearly vertical shaft on the slopes of a Mount Victorio. He climbed into the shaft and when he emerged a short time later, he had forgotten all about his hunting expedition. He went directly to his home and told his wife, Ova, that he had found an immense underground cave in which gold bars were stacked like cordwood. They weighed between fifty and seventy pounds each. He had two in his possession and told his wife he had removed eighty-six others before he had dynamited the cave entrance to hide it from other passing deer hunters. Apparently Noss lived from the proceeds of his find very well until after World War II. By that time, he had divorced Ova and she had remarried.

After the war, Noss entered into a partnership with Charles Ryan of Alice, Texas, to go back to the cave and reopen

123

the entrance. When he applied for a prospecting permit in the area, he discovered that his former wife had been issued an exclusive prospecting permit for a portion of the area by the New Mexico Land Office. Noss and Ryan, however, were granted another permit to prospect an area of Los Organos adjacent to the section reserved for Ova.

In the spring of 1949, Noss and Ryan set out for the cache, arranging for provisions and supplies to be air-dropped after their arrival. The plane bringing in the supplies was piloted by Curtis E. Noble of Albuquerque. The initial drop was scheduled for March 4, 1949, but as the plane neared the rugged mountain area for the rendezvous, it crashed. Noss pulled Noble and Marvin Beckwith, who was Noss' stepson, from the wreckage, placed them on mattresses in the back of the pickup truck and took them to a hospital in El Paso, where Noble was pronounced dead on arrival. Beckwith was seriously injured, but survived.

The next day, Noss met Ryan in Hatch, New Mexico, which is about halfway between El Paso and Hot Springs. The two men suddenly became embroiled in a furious argument, which ended when Ryan shot and killed Noss. Ryan was arrested and then released under $25,000 bond. During his preliminary hearing, Ryan said only that the argument arose over what he termed "illegal" use of Ryan's trucks. Ryan later was acquitted of the murder charges on the grounds that the killing was done in self-defense. He returned to Texas and, so far as is known, never returned to the area in which the cave is located.

Apparently Noss died keeping the exact location of the shaft a secret. Also kept secret was the location of the eighty-six gold bars he had hidden near the site before he dynamited the entrance. One of the bars he had taken to his home and the other, somehow, wound up in the possession of James Hurst, a United States Secret Service agent based in Albuquerque.

Mrs. Ova Noss still holds the prospecting rights in the

area, although a second Mrs. Noss has claimed that the treasure, if found, rightfully belongs to her. The prospecting rights are not doing Ova Noss much good, however, as the permit covers lands now embraced by the White Sands Proving Grounds and the military will allow no one to prospect in the area.

(The town of Hot Springs no longer is on the map. It was renamed Truth or Consequences after the producer of a radio quiz program by the same name agreed to originate the show there if the city council would change the name of the community.)

There is, however, no problem in searching around Trementina for the bars of gold that Juanita buried there near a church that later was used as a Presbyterian mission. The last inhabitant of Trementina departed in 1955.

A METEORIC LOSS

The thinly populated community of Port Orford, which lies astride a scenic coastal highway in southern Oregon, lends its name to a puzzling meteorological mystery. Few persons outside of Oregon ever have heard of this tiny community, yet any competent astronomer in any nation on this earth will nod knowingly when someone mentions the lost Port Orford Meteorite.

This is no ordinary rock from outer space. It is believed to be a portion of the huge Pallus Meteorite which fell into what now is Siberia a few thousand years ago. It has physical components unknown to present-day science and which have been discussed in innumerable scientific tracts. All over the Pacific Northwest there are stories that large rewards have been posted for its discovery. Although no one seems to know who is putting up the money, many searchers have spent months looking for this meteorite on the assumption that "Approximately one hundred tons of it lies above the ground in a timberless, grassy spot near Bald Mountain."

There is no question as to its existence. A fragment of it was chipped off in 1856 by Dr. John Evans, a government geologist, who was then exploring the little-known Oregon Territory. It was discovered by Evans on either the second or third night out from a trip which originated in Port Orford, and was scheduled to terminate either in an area which now is known as Gold Hill or in Roseberg.

On the night of the discovery, Evans made camp a little earlier in the afternoon than he had planned because of an unusual queasiness that he attributed to a mild form of indigestion. He next noticed that his compass was gyrating wildly and, then, a couple of members of his party were staggering as if they had been imbibing more than was good for them. None, however, would admit to drinking. Then others began to complain of stomach disorder. Shortly before dusk, one member of the exploration party walked away from the campsite about two hundred yards, stumbled and fell. He managed to get to his feet and stagger back to the camp where he felt somewhat better. A few minutes later, he went back toward the huge rock where he had fallen and once again he lost his balance and tumbled to the ground. This time Evans went to help him. As he neared the man, he was seized by an acute dizziness and felt himself stumbling around in a most unusual manner.

He helped the man back to the camp and as they moved away, their equilibrium was restored. There was no odor of a gas that could be affecting them, nor were they in a high enough altitude to be suffering from oxygen intoxication. They were in a large meadow, grassy but dry, that was ringed by timber. Off in the distance was a moderate-sized peak encrusted by snow that Evans had marked on his map as a Mount Baldy. The huge boulder rested in approximately the center of the meadow.

The men broke camp and moved back to the edge of the meadow, where presently they again felt normal. The following morning, Evans once again hiked toward the boulder. The closer he came to it, the more difficult he found it to control his movements. "It had the most strange effect upon the equilibrium," he wrote in his journal. Evans, however, managed to chip off a large portion of the boulder which he placed on one of the pack animals before resuming his journey.

Upon his return to Washington, several months later, Evans shipped the rock sample to the National Academy of Science in New York, headed by Dr. Charles T. Jackson, with a report of his strange experience. It was Jackson who made the discovery that the sample contained identical components, some unidentifiable, to the famed Pallus Meteorite of Russia. Jackson split the sample into two portions, kept one, and sent the other to the Academy of Science in Vienna, where his findings were confirmed. There appears to be no disagreement among scientists that this huge meteorite broke apart high over the Pacific, one portion falling in Oregon, the other in Siberia.

Because of its mysterious components, the Congress of the United States appropriated funds to finance another expedition to Oregon to relocate the meteorite. The expedition was to be headed by Jackson and Evans. At the time of the appropriation, however, Evans was in Central America on another exploration, where he died of "quick consumption" before the campaign could be launched.

Immediately before his death, he wrote to the National Academy of Science, "There cannot be the least difficulty in finding the meteorite. The western face of Bald Mountain, where it is, as its name indicates, bare of timber, is a grassy slope without projecting rock in the immediate vicinity of the meteorite. The mountain is a prominent landmark and can be seen from a long distance, as it is higher than any of the surrounding mountains."

Evans' death postponed the start of the expedition. Then it was delayed further by the outbreak of the Civil War. After the conclusion of this conflict, the Academy again appealed for federal funds to finance the expedition to Port Orford, but despite their pleas, the necessary money never was appropriated. No one has ever knowingly come across the meteorite since.

Richard Evans, a descendant of Dr. Evans, who lives in Washington, D.C., still has the daily journal kept by his great-grandfather during his exploration of the Oregon Territory. In it, there is a reference to "an oddly shaped tree with a huge boil on its trunk near where I camped and took a sampling of the strange rock."

About a three-day journey by horseback to the east of Port Orford and a short distance to the south is a tiny community known as Gold Hill. Many years ago there was a small gold mine there, but today Gold Hill is known for a curious phenomenon that exists a short distance beyond the town's limits. People going into this area outside of Gold Hill lose their equilibrium. Some have a slightly dizzy feeling and others stagger like drunks. Compasses spin wildly and watches lose all sense of time. Objects fall at an angle rather than straight down.

There are three mountains in the area, any one of which could qualify for the title of Mount Baldy, but it is unknown whether or not any tree that has a boil on its trunk exists in the area.

What is even more strange is the fact that apparently no one has ever wondered if Gold Hill is located on the lost Port Orford Meteorite. One possible answer for this is that no astron-

129

omer has ever visited Gold Hill and that no tourist who has visited Gold Hill ever has heard of the lost Port Orford Meteorite.

Other huge meteors have fallen in the West in Arizona and Nevada. What now is known as Big Soda Lake, five miles west of Fallon, Nevada, was created by a mile-long meteorite that slammed into the earth many years ago. If any meteorite ever struck near a populated area, the devastation probably would be total within fifteen miles, but the odds of such a happening are rather remote. The odds of such a bombardment from outer space striking a ship at sea are even more remote, yet many sailors believe this is what happened to the *Asiatic Prince* in the Pacific. It is one of the most mysterious disappearances in modern sea annals.

Built in 1926 for the Prince Line, the *Asiatic Prince* was a modern freighter under the command of a Captain Duncan. She carried a crew of forty-eight plus four apprentices. On March 16, 1928, she sailed from Los Angeles Harbor in late afternoon for Yokohama, Japan, and reportedly its cargo manifest listed a very large shipment of gold bullion and some arms and ammunition.

Shortly after dusk on the same evening, a man named Gordon Paynter happened to be on the west side of Santa Catalina Island when he saw a huge fireball in the sky. At first it appeared as a bright star, then it rapidly grew larger and larger, "a gigantic shooting star" that came right down into the sea, "rather than disappearing over the horizon or burning up as most do."

Other residents of the mainland in southern California, twenty-six miles to the east, also saw the shooting star and were impressed by the length of its voyage through the earth's atmosphere.

After the sighting of the "shooting star," the *Asiatic Prince* vanished. There was no radio contact either with shore or passing ship. The weather was good and the seas were relatively calm. It was the habit of Captain Duncan to maintain radio communications with land when he was at sea. Two days later, on March 18, agents for the Prince Line attempted to contact the freighter, but were unsuccessful.

At first it was thought that the ship's radio had failed and that Captain Duncan would put in at Honolulu to have it repaired.

Eight days later, a garbled SOS message was picked up from an unknown ship a few hundred miles west of Honolulu. Because the *Asiatic Prince* was known to be missing, it was thought that the message came from her, despite the fact that the call signs were not those of the missing ship. A futile search was launched in this area. More than a month later, a ship somewhere in the China Sea radioed that it was under attack by pirates and, probably because of the gold cargo, there were some who claimed that this was a distress call from the *Asiatic Prince*.

Lloyd's of London records indicate that the ship probably went down somewhere west of Hawaii, but there are few sailors who believe it. A fireball fell into the sea and from that moment on, the ship was never heard from again. There is another strange aspect to the disappearance of the *Asiatic Prince*.

It was a new ship of modern design. Many lives were lost. An exceptionally valuable cargo was lost. Yet there never was a formal investigation held as to the cause of its disappearance.

THE LOST TREASURE OF CUCAMONGA

The village of Cucamonga had been around for a long time before the coming of the white man, and it had survived without a curse or disappearing treasure. The land around the village was fertile, and the Cucamonga Indians lived an agrarian life, although they had their own efficient defense plans, so efficient that other tribes of marauding Indians never raided the Cucamongas.

When the padres came to the Mission San Gabriel, they reported that the Cucamongas "were unusually intelligent and industrious and were not easily managed."

The Cucamongas were not reluctant to learn from the padres. Within a short time after the Mission San Gabriel was opened, the Cucamongas were raising cattle and horses in addition to corn and melons. They tolerated the priests, but did not contribute as much to the establishment of the clerical hierarchy as did some of the other Indian tribes in the southern California area.

The tolerance lasted until 1839. In January of this year, Tiburcio Tapia, described as one of the leading citizens of Los Angeles, petitioned for a grant to the Cucamonga lands as an award for his devoted service. The grant was made on April 16 of the same year. The Cucamongas were not averse to being paid for building Don Tiburcio a huge adobe fortress on top of the highest hill in Cucamonga. When Don Tiburcio, however, indicated that the entire Cucamonga area was his domain and that henceforth the Cucamongas would be raising their crops and cattle for him, the Indians showed their displeasure by attacking the fortress they had built.

Don Tiburcio, anticipating this reaction, had brought in troops from Los Angeles and the Cucamongas were driven off their lands into the nearby foothills and canyons, where, for a number of years they continued to raid the fortress with such regularity that they virtually decimated themselves. The few that survived drifted away and more passive Indians were brought in to work the huge fields that Don Tiburcio gradually turned into vineyards running for miles in all directions from his fortress.

The suppression of the Cucamongas, however, did not herald a long era of peace and prosperity for Don Tiburcio. Less than five years after his grant had been awarded, Don Tiburcio realized that he faced an even more formidable enemy than the Cucamongas. This was the United States, which had made most clear its designs on Alta California. One of the precautions he took was to convert his Los Angeles holdings into gold coins and to hoard the earnings of his vineyards. Two large chests full of coins were kept hidden in the fortress and then, as the outbreak of war appeared inevitable, one of these chests was buried "somewhere near the west wing" of the mansion.

As happens on many occasions with hoarders, word of the

133

treasure spread around the countryside and eventually reached the attention of a Cucamonga Indian who decided that the money rightfully was his. His plan to acquire it was relatively simple. He applied for a job as a servant, was hired, and a couple of nights later was able to slip into Don Tiburcio's bedroom where he promptly slit Don Tiburcio's throat. While he was searching for the chests, he was surprised by the majordomo of the vineyard, who promptly shot him.

Don Tiburcio had one daughter, Maria Merced Tapia, who knew that another Indian in her father's employ actually had dug the hole where the chest was buried. The Indian agreed that he had indeed helped bury the chest, but he explained that Don Tiburcio had told him that he would die instantly if he revealed its location. The Indian had no intention of dying before his allotted time and no amount of persuasion could convince him that Don Tiburcio's curse was no longer any good. In exasperation, Maria Tapia had the servant thrown out of the fortress, fearful that he might overcome his fear of the curse and dig up the chest.

A few years later, Maria married a Leon V. Prudhomme, who moved into the fort. For the bridal chamber, they used the same room in which Don Tiburcio had been murdered. According to legend, on her wedding night Maria saw a small circle of light move across one of the adobe walls of the bedroom and rest on a particular spot. Her husband thrust a knife into the wall over the light and, quite to his surprise, found a small cavity in which was a purse of coins and a piece of paper so yellowed with age that no one could decipher the writing upon it. The few lines that were visible indicated that the paper was a crudely drawn map.

Maria and her husband lived in the fortress for approximately fifteen years, spending most of the time looking for the fortune her father had hidden. It was her inheritance and her dowry. Prudhomme apparently was no rancher and the couple lived by selling off portions of the land grant periodically to more capable ranchers. By 1858, they were down to less than two hundred acres, which they sold to John and Mercedes Rains, then they moved to Los Angeles.

Rains was an efficient businessman. He purchased more acreage which had been sold by Maria. He moved out of the old adobe mansion built by Don Tiburcio into a large brick house that he had built on a nearby hill. The fortress was allowed to crumble. He also raised cattle, built his own winery, and in short order was considered one of the wealthiest men east of Los Angeles in southern California. Rumors began to spread that Rains occasionally would display an old gold coin that was a part of Don Tiburcio's hoard. Word of this eventually reached the attention of Patrico Gonyllas, whose mother had been a Cucamonga Indian.

On the night of November 17, 1862, Gonyllas and his two sons paid a visit to John Rains and explained to him that the treasure rightfully was theirs. When Rains refused to divulge its location, the three of them dispatched Rains in the same manner as another Cucamonga Indian had disposed of the late Don Tiburcio.

This time there was no majordomo around to extract vengeance, but during the uproar, Mrs. Rains had disappeared, so the three murderers departed hastily. Two days later Gonyllas and his two sons slipped across the border into Baja California. No one knows where Gonyllas hid while he was in Baja California other than that it was somewhere in the vicinity of El Rosario.

Lewis Rawson, a descendant of early Californians, who presently owns a large ranch in Temecula, is the nephew of a woman who lived in El Rosario. Gonyllas came to her home on three or four different occasions to buy supplies and each time he paid for them with a "canteen full of mercury," telling her that

135

he had discovered a large pond of the quicksilver near his camp.

Today, mercury is becoming very scarce, thus expensive, and a pond of mercury would result in a fortune to its finder. It is found in cinnabar and is processed by a simple retort system. Rawson still has some of the mercury that was given to his aunt by the fugitive Gonyllas, and it is pure. In Baja California during the hot desert summer, the sun can vaporize the mercury on the cinnabar and when it cools, it can form in pools.

Gonyllas and his sons came back to the United States several months later. They were arrested when they crossed the border and all were hanged a short time later for the murder of John Rains. During his trial, which was brief, Gonyllas suggested that he would exchange the location of the mercury pond in return for a prison term for himself and his two sons. The offer was rejected. Mercury was only used in thermometers then, and there was plenty of it around.

Mercedes Rains married Jose C. Carrillo a few months after her husband's death. A short time later she sold the ranch. The old adobe winery built by Rains has been restored and is open for business. It is the oldest winery in California. The house where Rains was murdered now is a residence at 7869 Vineyard Avenue in Cucamonga. On the top of the adjacent hill is the site of the old fortress where Don Tiburcio was slain. The old fortress has disappeared and is now covered by homes and a portion of a golf course.

If the legend is correct, somewhere under one of those homes, or possibly under the eighteenth hole, is a fortune in gold coins.

THE LOST
SAINTS

Up until 1966, it was well established that there were twenty-one missions along the famed El Camino Real of the West and those who said there had been more were merely passing along myths. Then, in December of that year, the long-lost Santa Gertrudis Mission was found and now it is well established that there were twenty-two missions built along El Camino Real.

For years, there had been legends that there was a Santa Gertrudis Mission and explorers had hunted for it from the middle of Baja California to the outskirts of San Francisco. Historians and archivists, however, who had found obscure references to the missing mission believed that, if indeed, such a mission ever had existed, it lay buried in the Canada Larga, not far from the area where the Union Oil Company had brought in California's first oil gusher in 1888 on an 8000-acre ranch owned by Mrs. Mary Louise Canet.

There were no treasure tales connected with the Santa Gertrudis and thus the search for it had been conducted in a rather academic manner by scholars and in a haphazard manner by amateur archaeologists. In mid-1966, the California Highway Department disclosed plans to build still another superhighway between Los Angeles and Ventura, a portion of which would cut across the Canet Ranch.

About the same time Brother Henry, an archivist for the Christian Brothers Monastery in Napa, California, came across an early mission log from the San Buenaventura Mission, in Ventura, which referred to the Santa Gertrudis Mission.

"The governor has advised everyone in this mission (Santa Buenaventura) to retire to Santa Gertrudis because it is feared two ships carrying Peruvian insurgents are about to attack the community. We have packed everything that time will allow us to take along."

The report was written by a Father John Senan in 1818 and it described Santa Gertrudis Mission as being located about three leagues inland.

The two announcements were noticed by Roberta S. Greenwood, a southern California archaeologist, who also noticed that the new freeway would pass about three leagues east of the Santa Buenaventura Mission. With an associate, Robert O. Browne, of Ventura, she paid a call on the ninety-three-year-old owner of the ranch.

Mrs. Canet knew nothing about a lost Santa Gertrudis Mission. "I remember, however, there used to be a foundation and some walls standing out there in the bean field," she replied. She also recalled that one of the farmhands had found a large pot filled with old coins when he was plowing in the area.

138

The two archaeologists immediately set to work. Aided by a state grant, they managed to uncover the ruins of Santa Gertrudis along with a few assorted crucifixes and candlestick holders, before the freeway bulldozers arrived. The site presently is under about eighteen feet of gravel, asphalt, and cement.

The Santa Gertrudis Mission, which was found so soon before it was to become lost forever, was built by the Franciscans and the Franciscans apparently were less inclined to acquire treasures than were their brothers, the Jesuits.

It is the lost Jesuit missions around which the legends circulate, as they are believed to contain caches of incredible amounts of bullion, jeweled gold-and-silver icons. Recorded in the files of the Catholic Archdiocese of Mexico and on several old maps, crudely drawn but still in existence, are the names of several Jesuit missions that have become lost. One of the most famous is the Santa Isabel Mission, which was photographed as recently as 1922 in the Pajarito Mountains of Arizona and which is known to be a repository for Jesuit treasure which was hidden there shortly after the order was expelled from the New World by the king of Spain.

Another example is the lost Mission of San Dionysius. Its location is clearly marked, near Yuma, Arizona, on the banks of the Colorado River, by the cartographer Father Eusebio Francisco Chino, the mysterious Jesuit who is better known as Father Kino. One of Father Kino's diaries tells of his visit to this mission, yet today no one has been able to find any evidence of Mission San Dionysius.

The early missions of the West and Mexico were founded by the Jesuits and the archivists of the diocese also were Jesuits. In the mid-eighteenth century, this order found itself embroiled in a political situation when the king of Spain became suspicious of its increasing power and ordered all Jesuits expelled and replaced by the more docile Franciscans. Thus, it is understandable that the Jesuits, wishing to keep some of their more valuable possessions, hid them in missions such as the Santa Isabel and destroyed the records telling of their existence.

The Franciscans were more agrarian than clerical and, as in the case of the Santa Gertrudis Mission, their missions became lost primarily because no Franciscan padre ever bothered to note, except casually, that they had been built.

Still a different situation arises with the Dominicans. After the Mexicans passed the Secularization Act in 1833, the Dominicans were expelled because they were Spanish and most of them refused to take an oath of allegiance to the newly independent nation of Mexico. Most of the Dominicans unroofed their missions and departed as ordered. Their leaving was least lamented in Baja California. Here the priests had become so corrupt and greedy and powerful that they successfully defied the Dominican Order on the Mexican mainland.

The records of the Catholic Diocese in Mexico contain countless reports of brutal conduct by the maverick Baja Dominican friars against the Indians, of carousing, wenching, and theft. In 1803, the Dominican Order requested soldiers to forcibly remove and exile the superior of the Baja California mission for misconduct, along with some priests at the Loreto Mission. Shortly before the Mexican revolution the Dominican Order heard that their Baja California brothers were operating a gold mine and smelter with slave labor, that the mine was called the Santa Clara Mission and that the gold was being shipped out through the harbor now known as Scammons Lagoon. Once again they asked for military help, but this time none was forthcoming because of the emergency attending the revolution. The alleged mission was described as being west of San Ignacio and north of Bahia Ballenas. There was a church near the mine, the report stated, that "bore no cross on its peak" but could be recognized by the statues of five monks set in niches along the face of the building.

It took many months for word of the expulsion order to

reach the carousing Dominicans at Santa Clara. When the message did arrive, it came only a week before the soldiers were scheduled to arrive at the various Baja California missions to escort them out. The priests, with their slave labor, worked desperately, but efficiently. Hundreds upon hundreds of gold bars were buried a short distance from the secreted church. Not so easily hidden, however, were several hundred pounds of gold dust. It could not be buried loosely. There were no containers available that would not rot in the ground very quickly. According to the legend, however, this group of maverick priests had prepared for such an emergency. Each of the five monks in the niches of the church was a hollow statue and each one was filled with several hundred pounds of valuable gold dust. The Indians then were told to take the statues to their villages, to keep them in a place of honor and to treat each statue as a saint, as a symbol of their faith, until the Dominicans returned. Anyone who did not treat these saints in a most reverent manner would incur the full wrath of the Lord.

When this was accomplished, the friars dismantled the smelter, covered up the entrance to the mine, deroofed the church and departed for their respective missions to await the soldiers. Several years later, one of these maverick priests apparently regretted his evil ways in Baja California and made a full report of the incident to his superiors in Spain. A copy of the report made its way back across the Atlantic to the diocese in Mexico City, where it was filed and forgotten because no record of a Santa Clara Mission could be found in the church library. Many years later, a La Paz priest wrote to ask the location of the "lost Santa Clara Mission" which he had been told was somewhere on the Baja California Peninsula. This request apparently was filed and unanswered.

Early in 1900, two North American adventurers and prospectors named Ulysses Andreson and William Williams rode into

141

a small ranch some miles southwest of San Ignacio in a mountain range known as the Santa Claras. Five statues, each about six feet tall, were lined up in the yard. One was being painted by a Mexican and Andreson noticed that a woman with Indian features who passed close by them crossed herself as she looked toward the idols. Andreson went closer, then moved back as he sensed a sudden hostility from the Mexican who was doing the painting.

The two North Americans moved out of the village and camped. The next morning, they discovered a rich vein of gold near where they had slept. There is no record of the two men discovering a mine shaft or the ruins of an old mission. Andreson and Williams worked the lode until they had as much ore as they could carry out on burros purchased from the natives. The vein was so worked out that they did not think it worthwhile to return.

A few years later, an expedition from the National Academy of Science, headed by Edward Goldman and Edward Nelson, was exploring the southern Baja California area. Goldman made a side trip into the Santa Clara Mountains searching for antelope and jaguar. In his report, he wrote that on the other side of the Vizcaino Desert, about fifty miles from San Ignacio, he came across a small village with a "fine tank of good water" on the western side of the Santa Clara Mountains. "There is evidence of placer mining in the mountains here," he said. He makes no reference to any saints.

In 1922, a Mexican writer-explorer wrote of a trip he made through the area. He also refers to signs of placer mining and a "deserted village" adjacent to the mine. He advances no theory as to why the village had been abandoned nor does he mention the saints. The next known mention of them occurs about ten years later when a British journalist named Frank Newman arrived in Black Warrior, in Baja California to write a

142

story of the mating of the huge gray whales in Scammons Lagoon, which is nearby.

He wrote of seeing four large statues of priests about six feet tall "so heavy that it requires a half-dozen strong men to lift one. Despite their weight and somewhat grotesque appearance, they travel from one isolated community to another to commemorate some religious fiesta. Their origin is somewhat of a mystery."

They were next noticed by Mrs. Barbara Edwards of Whittier, California, who was visiting Santo Domingo, many miles to the north of Scammons Lagoon. "They are about three feet high," she said, "and require five men to lift each one. Originally there were five, but now there are only four, as one was loaned to a neighboring village for a celebration and never was returned."

According to Mrs. Edwards, the guardian of the saints was the eldest resident of the village, a patriarch who proudly pointed them out to her in a shed in back of his house. Mrs. Edwards disagreed with Newman. "They are perfectly beautiful," she said.

The day before Easter in 1964, the police in Enseñada, Baja California, a tourist city about sixty-five miles below San Diego, were called to a Catholic church. The priest was sad. About a week earlier, some residents of Santa Domingo had, at great expense and hardship, trucked four statues of great weight to the church to be displayed during the religious holidays. They had been in custody of the village for many years and, although somewhat primitive in appearance, they obviously were of great value to the villagers. The men of the village referred to them as saints, the priest said, and they would be returning to pick them up on the day after Easter. Unfortunately, someone had stolen two of them.

The priest pointed out the two remaining ones at the sides of the church doors. All four were alike, he said, and although they were excellent examples of primitive art, they were too heavy to be easily stolen by a gringo souvenir hunter. The two police officers tried to lift one of the statues and agreed with the priest.

The search at first concentrated around Enseñada. No one could be found who had seen them taken. No one around the church had heard anything unusual the night before. The police in Tijuana were notified, and in turn contacted the border patrol station in the United States. A customs officer recalled a pickup truck crossing the border about two in the morning with two statues in the bed of the truck. He was shown a picture and he thought they were similar. He recalled there were three people in the cab of the truck; two men and a young girl with long blond hair. They were United States citizens. The statues, they said, had been purchased for five dollars from a clutter shop in Tijuana.

The Mexican state police in Baja California reported the theft to the U.S. border patrol and the FBI, and it was routinely logged by other law enforcement agencies in southern California.

One of the more popular sports in southern California is dune bugging. A dune bug is a small compact vehicle with exceptionally large tires that will travel like a fast tractor over the sand dunes and the deserts of the area. Addicts will tow their dune bugs from the cities, park by the side of a lonely road and then drive for miles across the desert, exploring, prospecting, or just driving for the thrills of climbing a large sandy dune. There is a law in California that any passenger car towing a trailer cannot exceed a speed limit of fifty-five miles per hour.

Approximately one week after the theft of the saints from the Enseñada church, a California Highway Patrol car gave chase to a sports car towing a dune bug that was traveling about seventy miles per hour on a wide highway between Palm Springs and Indio. Inside the sports car was a young married couple from Los

144

Angeles. Propped inside the dune bug was an old wooden statue of a saint or a priest.

The patrolman wrote out a speeding ticket to the driver and then, suddenly remembering the report of the stolen saints, went back to look at the statue. The driver of the sports car went with him. "I found it in the sand just off one of the back roads near Palm Desert," he explained.

"Is it heavy?"

"Not very."

The patrolman discovered that he could lift the statue with one hand. The stolen property report described the saints as being extraordinarily heavy. He waved the driver on his way. A few hours later, however, after his return to his station, he reported the incident to the FBI. A day or so later, an FBI agent called upon the couple in their surburban Los Angeles home. The statue was in a patio with a straw hat over its head.

With the hat removed, the statue matched the description of one of the saints stolen, except that the agent could pick it up easily.

"There was another one like it near where we found this," the man volunteered. "It was about fifty yards farther down the road. Apparently there had been a sandstorm and the other one was partially buried in a dune. Besides, we didn't have room to carry it." The man had no objection to turning the statue over to the FBI.

A day after this the FBI found the second statue near Palm Desert. This one also was light and the base of the statue was at right angles to the first one. It was not difficult to guess that they had been thrown into the sand from a passing truck. Unless one stopped, they would appear as a log or a discarded fence post. It also was easy to determine why the statues had lost so much weight. The bases screwed off and the interiors were hollow. Whatever had been inside had been removed.

145

Both statues were dusted for fingerprints, but none were found. A short time later they were taken to the border at Tijuana and turned over to the Mexican state police who, in turn, took them back to the church in Ensenada. The other two statues no longer were on the church steps. The men from Santo Domingo had taken them back to their village.

There is an aftermath to the story that cannot be verified. The priest, who was a wise and understanding man, was concerned over the reaction from the Indians when they discovered that their saints weighed much less when they were returned than when they had been donated for the Easter holidays. Accordingly, he instructed his acolytes to fill them up with sand before they were returned to Santo Domingo.

The location of the four heavy saints now is unknown, except to a few elders of the village of Santo Domingo. When asked, the elders have replied evasively that they have been loaned to another village for a fiesta. But somewhere in northern Baja California are four wooden saints, two of them loaded with sand from the beaches of Ensenada, and two others quite probably loaded with gold dust worth a fortune that was taken from the old Santa Clara Mission mines. In some village, somewhere in that mysterious seven-hundred-mile-long peninsula, quite probably is still another saint, also loaded with gold dust, which really is not dust at all, but pure gold sand.

146

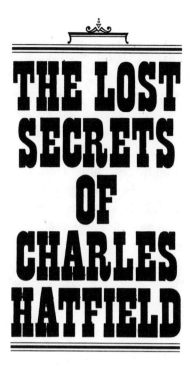

THE LOST SECRETS OF CHARLES HATFIELD

The late Adolf Spreckels did well in sugar but he was not worth a dam in water. Around the turn of the century, southern California was in the throes of a long drought. The city of San Diego was going through a population boom and there were justifiable fears that if the water shortage lasted much longer, the boom would dry out.

Spreckels, one of the most prominent members of the community, banded together a group of the city's more prosperous businessmen in an effort to solve the problem. Engineers and surveyors were hired and told to find quickly the most practical spot for a dam to be built to hold the water for a new reservoir for the city.

Some weeks later, agreement was reached on the site for construction of the Morena Dam. It was located sixty miles east of San Diego in the Cuyamaca Mountains near the Mexican border. From both an engineering and geological point of view, it was an excellent location. It was at the head of a small lake fed by a stream and the dam would fit nicely between the walls of a steep canyon. Funds were raised from private sources to buy the property and finance the major part of the construction costs. Before the first spadeful of earth was turned on the project, title to the dam and the surrounding area was turned over to the city, as a public gesture.

It takes time to build a dam. Long before it was completed, workmen noticed that the lake was getting smaller and that the stream that fed it was getting narrower. Still, there was a general air of optimism. The drought could not possibly last much longer and when it ended, the lake would fill and provide a reservoir that would meet all of San Diego's needs for at least a half-century or more. Two years later, when the completion ceremonies were held, the optimism was less noticeable. The lake was more than one hundred yards from the base of the dam and the stream that fed it was little more than a trickle. A short time after the dedication ceremonies, the lake had turned to a marshy meadow and the stream was nonexistent.

By 1912, the water shortage had become acute. In that year, a real estate agent named F. A. Binney and a delegation from the San Diego Wide Awake Improvement Club approached the city council with the suggestion that it hire Charles M. Hatfield to come down and produce a little rain. Hatfield was a rainmaker of no small reputation, but the city council told Binney and the members of the Wide Awake Improvement Club that it doubted Hatfield's talents were sufficiently advanced to warrant any spending of the taxpayers' money upon such frivolity.

Binney, however, believed in Hatfield as strongly as a

148

flying saucer fan believes in visitors from outer space and he kept returning to the council with his proposal. There was some justification for the council's skepticism, because Hatfield was only a part-time rainmaker. His main source of income came from commissions he made selling sewing machines in California. He and his brother Paul had been born in the Midwest but had been brought by their parents to California when they were children. They had settled near Vista, in San Diego County, at the start of the long drought. With the help of their father, they had built a platform of some twenty feet in the back yard of their farm, placed a windmill on it, then whipped up a batch of chemicals which they blew into the cloudless sky. A short time later, Vista was treated to a light rain, which was the only place it rained that day in southern California.

The skeptics were not convinced, so the Hatfields made up a slightly stronger potion and blew it into the sky on a day when there was not a cloud in sight. This time, Vista got .65 of an inch and no one else got a drop. The Hatfield fan club began to grow.

The Los Angeles Chamber of Commerce offered Hatfield one thousand dollars if he could make it rain in the city. Hatfield built a new tower in the vicinity of Baldwin Hills and blew the fumes from his chemicals into the sky for four months. Los Angeles measured eighteen inches of rain, while San Diego didn't get a drizzle. The chamber finally asked him to quit his operations because the tourists were complaining about the long siege of rain and clouds. The chamber cheerfully paid Hatfield the stipulated fee.

His reputation as a rainmaker spread far and wide. In 1915, the Denver *Post* devoted nearly an entire page to his talents as a rainmaker. He filled a lake in Stanislaus County, California, and a reservoir in Fresno. Still, the parched city council in San Diego steadfastly refused to hire the rainmaker, despite the insistence of the indignant Binney and the Wide Awake Improvement Club.

Early in December of 1915, a delegation from the Wide Awake Improvement Club journeyed to Eagle Rock, a suburb of Los Angeles, and implored Hatfield to turn his attention toward San Diego. Hatfield, apparently, was touched because, on December 8, 1915, the city council received a letter from him in which he offered to produce forty inches of rain around Morena Dam at no expense to the city.

"What have we got to lose?" Binney cried out to the council, after the letter was read.

For the first time the councilmen agreed with Binney. They ordered City Clerk Allen H. Wright to send a telegram to Hatfield asking him to attend a council meeting on the following day.

Hatfield showed up with a written proposition. "I will fill the Morena Reservoir to overflowing between now and next December 20, 1916, for the sum of ten thousand dollars, in default of which I ask no compensation: or I will deliver at Morena Reservoir thirty inches of rain at no charge, you to pay me five hundred dollars per inch from the thirteenth inch to the fiftieth inch—all above fifty-inches to be free, on or before the first of June, 1916. Or I will discharge forty inches during the next twelve months, free of charge, provided you pay me $1000 per inch for all between forty and fifty inches, all above fifty inches free."

The city council told Hatfield to go ahead and fill up the reservoir for a flat fee of $10,000. Binney and the Wide Awake Improvement Club cheered and Hatfield accepted the directive as a contract. A few days later, he and his brother, Paul, started to build their platforms on a high hill near the Morena Dam. This time, they did not use the windmill. Instead, they built in a well-protected brick fireplace on the platform, laid in a huge supply of firewood, and stewed their chemicals over the fire. The first wisp of smoke from the potions rose into the air on Thursday, January 13.

Thirteen days earlier, the famed Agua Caliente Racetrack had opened its doors, just across the United States-Mexico border. The daily attendance averaged around 10,000 fans. Additional thousands of tourists were in San Diego attending an exposition in Balboa Park.

On Friday, January 14, black clouds began to form early in the morning over Morena Dam. By noon, it was pouring so hard that the races at Agua Caliente were called off. The tourists remained away from the exposition. The rivers began to fill. City Attorney T. B. Cosgrove nervously remembered the Hatfields.

"While it obviously is raining hard," he told a San Diego reporter, "and although obviously the runoff is pouring into the Morena Reservoir, no money should be paid until it is determined that this is the direct result of Mr. Hatfield's efforts."

By the following Monday morning, the rain still was falling in sheets. The situation was becoming serious. Part of the Agua Caliente Racetrack washed away. Dry rivers had risen so rapidly that several smaller bridges were washed out. The secondary roads were impassable and rail communication to the north was shut off.

Charles Hatfield called the San Diego city hall to report that he had accumulated 12.78 inches of rain. "I just wanted to tell you that this is only a sprinkle. Within the next few days, I expect it to rain right."

Hatfield apparently was very serious. By January 20, it was still pouring. A Sante Fe passenger train was marooned near Oceanside, a few miles north of San Diego, and the passengers finally were removed by a seagoing launch. More than one hundred homes were washed out in Tijuana and the city building

151

department reported that it would cost about three-hundred-thousand dollars just to replace the bridges that had been washed out. An attempt was made to reach Hatfield by telephone, but the lines had been washed out. A party was sent on horseback to the Morena Dam.

The Hatfields were still in their house on top of one of the platforms and the smoke and fumes from their fires still boiled upward into the sky. One member of the party, no one remembers his name, climbed up the ladder and said the city would immediately pay him ten thousand dollars to shut off his machine. Hatfield thought the offer a reasonable one, doused his fires and removed his chemicals. Approximately a half hour later, the rain stopped.

Two days later, a happy and well-groomed Charles Hatfield appeared before the city council and presented it with a bill for ten thousand dollars. Cosgrove shook his head. The man who had made the offer had no authority to speak for the city. Under the deal, Hatfield was to be paid only if he filled the Morena Reservoir to overflowing and, according to witnesses who had gone out to the dam, it was only about half full.

It was an angry Charles Hatfield who left city hall, still carrying his unaccepted bill for services rendered. He was still angry when he got back to his platforms and he apparently was still angry when he mixed up his chemicals once again, for this time he made them stronger than ever.

On January 24, it started to rain again. This time the deluge did, indeed, make the earlier storms appear as mere sprinkles. The ground could hold no more rain. It poured down the sides of the hills and the mountains, flash flooding through canyons into riverbeds that spilled out into the coastal mesas before the ocean. Even the banks of the dry rivers collapsed before the incredible surge of water. The coast road to Los Angeles was washed out, as was the railroad tracking between

152

the two cities. Railroad officials covered one rail bridge with a dozen loaded freight cars on the theory that their weight would prevent the bridge from falling. Both bridge and rail cars were washed out to the shore of the sea. Ships were swept from their moorings in the bays and almost all telephone communication was severed. A dam in Switeear Canyon in back of Balboa Park showed signs of giving away and, for some reason, city engineers decided to help it collapse by setting off a huge charge of dynamite at its base. This wave of water alone took several San Diego homes out to sea. Another large dam, known as Sweetwater, split without warning and still another disastrous wall of water swept down toward the city. A few hours later, a dam holding back a reservoir known as Lower Otay Lake simply vanished under the pressure of the water. In addition to countless homes, this wall of water wiped out a 3000-foot section of track of the San Diego & Arizona Railroad, which was owned largely by Spreckels, who had been responsible for the construction of Morena Dam where the Hatfields were working so diligently.

On January 26, the city council dispatched another delegation to seek peace with the Hatfields, but this group now was unable to get through to the platforms. They did bring back a message from the caretaker at Morena Dam. The water level behind the dam had risen eighteen feet within the past two days.

On the following day, the last of the homes in the Tia Juana River Valley were swept out to sea. The known dead counted more than twenty. United States Marines were alerted to prevent looting from mercantile establishments that still were left standing, although knocked from their foundations. A residential area known as Little Lander was obliterated. Still Hatfield continued sending his chemicals into the storm-swollen skies, and still the incredible deluge continued.

On January 29, the Morena Dam caretaker sent word that the water level at the dam was less than a foot from the top and that he had observed Hatfield studying the top of the dam with a pair of binoculars. Shortly before the following noon, the water began to spill over the top of Morena Dam. An hour later, it was cascading down its face like a waterfall. A short time after this, the caretaker noticed that smoke no longer was rising from the Hatfield platforms. By late afternoon, the rains were over. At Morena Dam, the skies were blue and the few clouds that were in the sky were a puffy white.

The Hatfield brothers climbed down from their platform and went to the caretaker's home to pick up their horses, but the caretaker indignantly refused to return them "because of all the trouble they had caused."

The Hatfields set out on foot for San Diego, approximately sixty miles distant. "We were amazed at the damage," Paul Hatfield later told reporters. "We expected a little flooding, but nothing so much as we saw."

The Hatfields realized, also, that they were not very popular when, on the following morning, they met a group of farmers armed with axes and pitchforks heading up the trail to chop down the platforms and "to spear them damn Hatfields like a forkful of hay." Both Hatfields were invited to join the foray, but they declined, identifying themselves as the Benson brothers who had been wiped out by the floods.

On the morning of February 6, Charles Hatfield met with reporters in the real estate offices of Binney. One reporter said he acted like "a proverbial conquering hero, home from the fray and awaiting a laurel wreath." Hatfield said he was in no manner responsible for the loss of life and damage caused by the storm. "I entered into a contract with the city and it was up to the city to take the necessary precautions."

The city council also was in a rather unfriendly mood. Cosgrove made it most clear that the stipulated $10,000 fee would not be paid. He explained his reasoning behind the refusal. If the City of San Diego paid Hatfield anything, then it would be assuming liability for all of the damage caused by the floods. The resulting suits and claims would run into millions. In addition, he added, there was no way that Hatfield could prove that he had been responsible for the rain, a point which was indeed fortunate for Hatfield, otherwise he would be target for the suits and damage claims.

Hatfield did not quite see the matter in the same vein as Cosgrove. The two brothers went back to Eagle Rock, from where they sent repeated demands for payment of the promised fee. In December of 1916, Hatfield sued San Diego for $400,000. In a preliminary hearing, Cosgrove pointed out that no contract had been signed with Hatfield, but that the city was willing to settle for the full amount provided Hatfield would assume responsibility for the 3.5 million dollars in lawsuits that had been filed against the city for hiring the rainmaker.

Hatfield said he would think it over. Six months later he offered to settle the whole affair for $1800, which he said was less than his expenses incurred in the project. Cosgrove was not even interested in this bargain price. Hatfield did not pursue it. He was worried about being sued himself, although as near as can be determined, no suit ever was filed against him. His suit against the city remained on the court docket until 1938, when it was quietly dismissed "as a dead issue."

The San Diego experiment marked the end of the rainmaking career of Charles Hatfield, although in the ensuing years he was offered several opportunities to apply his talents in areas ranging from Texas to South America. The deals always fell through when Hatfield asked for a substantial retainer in advance. He died quietly in Los Angeles in 1952 and none of the obituary writers commented on his remarkable talent for producing rain.

His brother, Paul, still lives in a Los Angeles suburb. "Sure he could make rain," he says. "We just stumbled on a secret that someone else will find someday. They already are getting close to the idea by seeding clouds to make rain and seeding clouds to disperse fog.

"They have had a lot of meteorological experts who have studied the San Diego case and have come up with the story that it rained in Oregon and Washington the the same time we brought the rain to San Diego. Hell, it always rains in Oregon and Washington. But don't overlook the fact that it hadn't rained in San Diego for years before we went to work, it didn't rain again for a couple of years after we left."

Paul Hatfield does not know the formula, however. His brother kept that to himself. When he died, the secret potions of Hatfield the Rainmaker were lost forever.

LOST
IN LAVA

In the central northwest section of New Mexico there is an extinct volcano known as Mount Taylor that is as treacherous today as it was when it first spewed its molten lava for many miles to the south. It towers more than 11,000 feet into the sky from the high mesa on which it is rooted, and it has been a source of fatal fascination to many an unwary airman because of the heavy downdrafts that sweep down its slopes. The wreckage of many a light plane lies in the deep crevasses of the long lava flow, along with military aircraft from the Second World War. It was on the lava flow from Mount Taylor that the flamboyant motion picture producer Mike Todd met his death in an air

157

crash. Somewhere nearby is believed to be the wreckage of an oil company's courier airplane that crashed during the late thirties while ferrying a reported $100,000 from Los Angeles to New York.

The area is one of the most mysterious in the American Southwest. Nearby dwelt one of the most ancient, and certainly one of the strangest, communities in all of the Americas. Built hundreds of years before Coronado made his trek to the north to search for the seven cities of Cíbola, the town of Acoma rests atop a 400-foot-high mesa that juts as abruptly out of the ground as does a New York skyscraper. Access can be gained only by ladders or by climbing up niches carved out of the face of the cliff, yet on the top of this huge, remote cliff, are terraced adobe homes, some three stories tall, and the largest mission church in New Mexico. Nothing grows in Ácoma. Everything from water to firewood is hauled up the face of the cliff, yet at one time this was the home of more than 6,000 persons.

When Coronado's soldiers first came to Ácoma and scaled the cliffs to enter the town, they were welcomed, but the feeling of camaraderie did not last for long. In 1598, the Ácomans bludgeoned the Spaniards into a state of semiconsciousness, then tossed them over the cliffs to the rocks below. Some years later, after the Franciscans had arrived at the town, the Ácomans once again lost their temper and tossed the padres over the cliffs.

Other Spaniards and other monks came, however, and around 1700, work on the huge mission church was started. The walls are more than 60 feet high and 10 feet thick. The ceiling beams for the edifice are about 40 feet long and 14 inches square and came from mountains more than twenty-five miles distant. All of the materials were carried up by the Indians.

There was reason for the intense Spanish interest in Ácoma. They were convinced that it was indeed one of the seven cities of Cíbola. According to the legend in Mexico City,

Montezuma told Cortes that much of the silver of the Aztecs came from the distant city of Ácoma, a city on a cliff near the black hills where the silver mine was located. If there was a mine in the lava flow, the Spaniards never found it and neither has anyone else.

Not far from Ácoma is the Enchanted Mesa, which is much smaller and rises even higher than Ácoma. The walls are even more sheer here and, again, according to legend, this was at one time the residence for the leaders of the Ácoman society. It is possible to get to the top of the Enchanted Mesa through a "chimney" in approximately the center of the cliff, although it is a most arduous climb. One archaeologist who did make the climb found many artifacts to prove that Ácomans actually did live on the top of the Enchanted Mesa. It was abandoned abruptly, the Ácomans say, after an earthquake, followed by another eruption from Mount Taylor. So quick was the departure that three Ácoman women were left behind. One jumped off and was killed. The other two perished from starvation. For many, many years, it was impossible to get to the top of the Enchanted Mesa, but then there was another earthquake and the chimney was opened.

There are many who believe that the cliff-dwelling Ácomans took to their high perch to avoid the lava flow from Mount Taylor, and that prior to this, there was a large city on the flat land below. There are consistent unattributable reports that at the bottom of some of the deep crevasses in the huge lava flow can be seen traces of homes and buildings, and there are some who believe that this was the site of the fabled Azatlán, the city from which the Aztecs originally came.

In 1882, when the Santa Fe Railroad was being constructed west of Albuquerque, workers digging through the lava flow unearthed three large pottery ollas around which the lava had flowed. In each olla was a human skeleton. The discovery was printed in an Albuquerque newspaper of July 27 of that year, but no mention was made as to the disposition of either the ollas or the skeletons. A few days later, the workers came across another olla. A supervisor noticed the men gathered around the discovery and confiscated the olla. Inside he found three Spanish coins, all dated 1543. Whether or not there were more that were divided up among the workers before his arrival has never been determined. In 1950, highway workers cutting an improved road through the lava flow came across a small iron chest which contained about $10,000 in Confederate paper money. The iron chest was rather badly rusted, but the paper was in excellent condition, despite the fact that its purchasing power was nil. Most think it was thrown away by fleeing Confederate soldiers as worthless baggage at the conclusion of the Civil War.

The lava flow stretches for many miles in all directions south of Mount Taylor. The crevasses are deep, sometimes wide and twisting. During World War II, the pilot of a medium-range bomber, who was on a training mission, radioed Kirtland Field in Albuquerque that he was having engine trouble. He gave his location as approximately one mile south of Mount Taylor. The plane was never seen or heard from again.

In 1947 one of these writers, while piloting a small plane over the area, spotted the olive drab empennage of a bomber lying on top of the lava about four miles south of Grants. The color blended so closely with the black lava that it was visible only from an altitude of about one hundred feet. Somewhere nearby in one of the lava canyons lies the rest of the missing plane.

The writer who found the tail of the missing bomber was looking for a different aircraft, a single-engine Lockheed Vega that is believed to have gone down in the treacherous lava beds in 1936. This latest legend of Mount Taylor and its lava flow is tied into the election contest of that year between Franklin D. Roosevelt and Kansas Governor Alf Landon.

Shortly before the election, there were several rumors that Mexico was planning to expropriate the United States oil companies operating in that nation and that Roosevelt, in the interests of his "Good Neighbor" policy, was not going to protest the action so long as the oil companies received a reasonable payment for their investment. The oil companies felt that Landon would take a stronger position against the pending expropriation if he was elected and Landon, whose chances for winning were not rated very high, desperately needed campaign funds. The oil industry in California raised $100,000 from among its members for a Landon donation.

As is the custom in many political donations, the money was raised in cash. It was urgently needed by the appropriate Republican campaign officials in New York and thus, a pilot by the name of Touchmann was hired in Los Angeles as a courier to fly the money to New York. He took off from Burbank, California, in a red Lockheed Vega, after telephoning ahead to a privately operated airport in Albuquerque to request that it remain open until his arrival so he might refuel. He was assured that it would.

Shortly before dusk of the same day, an insurance man and pilot from Albuquerque, named Homer Bray, who was flying to Gallup, noticed a red Lockheed Vega far below him. Bray had just passed over the western edge of the lava flow, a few miles below San Fidel, and was approaching the Cíbola National Forest. From where he was, it appeared that the Vega was skimming the ground. A few seconds later it occurred to Bray that the pilot of the Vega might be in trouble. Bray's first thought was that the strange pilot was going to be in a hell of a lot more trouble if he were heading for a forced landing in the lava beds. Bray made a 180-degree turn and dropped down for a second look. He could see no sign of the Vega.

Bray was flying a Bellanca, a much slower plane than a Vega, and after he had flown back about twenty or thirty miles

161

without seeing the other aircraft, he decided that the plane was probably in no trouble and that its low altitude had merely been an optical illusion. It was not until he returned to Albuquerque the following day that he learned a red Lockheed Vega had disappeared on a flight between Phoenix and Albuquerque.

Bray reported what he had seen and led an aerial search party to the area later that afternoon. There was no sign of the aircraft. If it had crashed in the lava beds, it was unlikely that there ever would be, as both Bray and the other local pilots well knew.

Nevertheless, the search was carried on for two more days before it was abandoned. About three days after this, a well-dressed young man who was highly articulate and said he was a private detective from Los Angeles came into Bray's office. His name, the detective said, was Roger Smith, and he was most interested in locating the wreckage of the missing Vega. He said he represented a group of California businessmen who would pay all expenses for another air search of the area, and a $5,000 bonus if the plane was located. He advanced Bray $1,000, a considerable sum in mid-Depression days, to meet his immediate costs and said he would be available for any reports at the Alvarado Hotel.

Bray told his visitor that if the plane was down in the lava beds, the odds were a thousand to one that it would be found, but Smith was prepared to accept the risk.

Once again an aerial search was launched, this time with more than a dozen planes taking part. The search went on for a week. Every night, Bray met Smith in the bar of the old Alvarado Hotel. He soon learned that the visitor was not a professional private detective and that his name was not really Smith. He discovered also that Smith could not hold his liquor very well.

On the night the second search was called off, Bray and his companion had three or four martinis at the Alvarado. "This plane seems to have some extraordinary importance," Bray said.

162

Smith nodded, then looking around him, he lowered his voice and told Bray the story. When he was finished, he sat back and ordered another round of drinks.

"Thank you for trusting me with your confidence," Bray said, wondering whether or not the stranger was telling him the truth.

The man shrugged. "It is really nothing," he replied. "It would be denied by everyone, even if you told it."

"If I tell everyone, then everyone will be out looking for the plane."

The pseudo-Smith laughed. "Wait until I get back to Los Angeles," he replied.

Bray, who was a strong Democrat, told New Mexico's Senator Dennis Chavez. The Senator thought the story probably was true, but agreed with the mysterious Smith that if it was told, it would be denied. In addition, if it was made public, it might backfire because the Democrats would be accused of resorting to "smear politics." He asked Bray to keep it quiet.

Two years later, the Mexican government did expropriate the United States-owned oil companies in Mexico and, as Smith had predicted, Roosevelt made no protest. Bray spent some time cruising over the lava beds and the adjacent Ácoma Reservation and the Cíbola National Forest, but he could find no sign of the missing aircraft.

The war kept him busy for the next few years and the mystery was stored in the back of his mind. Shortly after the end of the war, however, he was reminded of it forcibly. General Patrick J. Hurley was running for a New Mexico senate seat against Clinton Anderson. One evening, during the campaign, Bray was in the lobby of the Hilton Hotel when Hurley entered the building. With Hurley was the mysterious pseudo-Smith. When Smith saw Bray, he stared at him for a moment, then smiled slightly, nodded, and turned his attention back to the general. It was most obvious that he did not wish to renew the acquaintanceship any further. The insurance executive asked several people around the lobby if they knew who the man was, but none of the local politicians ever had seen him before. All that Bray could learn was that the man had accompanied Hurley on a flight from Los Angeles earlier in the day.

Bray no longer kept the story quiet. He was a colonel in the Civil Air Patrol and on several occasions he led members on a search expedition of the lava flow, but with no success. For several years, amateur pilots have been making passes over the lava beds looking for the lost Lockheed Vega, which surely is buried in one of the steep twisting fissures of the black rock. If anyone has found it, he has kept the discovery quiet.

Some day, the wreckage of the plane surely will turn up, like the tail from the lost bomber, like the iron chest full of Confederate money, like the ancient coins of Coronado's era and the three skeletons in the large ollas.

A TRIO OF LOST MONSTERS

Apparently the first genuine sea serpent ever sighted by a man not in his cups was seen by an aging cleric named Bishop Pontoppidan off the shores of Bergen, Norway, back in 1734. The good bishop was a teetotaler, was well respected in his parish, and when he told of seeing a sea serpent more than one hundred feet long less than fifty yards from the shore, where he was meditating, enough of his flock believed in him to mount a long watch in hopes of glimpsing it. The bishop's sea serpent apparently was a transient because it was never seen around Bergen again. When the insistent bishop referred to the serpent as a heavenly manifestation in one of his sermons, some of his more stolid parishioners reached the conclusion that the cleric was well past the retirement age and suggested that he go back to his meditation along the seashore on a more permanent basis. Thus, the Reverend Pontoppidan occupies the unique position of not only being the first person to see a sea serpent, but the only person ever to be damaged in any manner by these monsters of the deep.

Shortly after the good bishop reluctantly acceded to the wishes of his parishioners, however, sightings of the elusive sea serpents became more common. One of the best chronicled sightings was that of a monstrous sea reptile that cavorted for two weeks in Gloucester Harbor, Massachusetts, in 1817 before hundreds of skeptical New Englanders. Scientists even came from distant Boston to view the antics of the strange beast, but if their conclusions were ever published, they have long since been lost.

It was off the coast of the Western United States, however, that the aging Bishop Pontoppidan finally was cleared of senility charges almost two hundred years later. Not only were a mother and child sea serpent sighted, but the baby was captured and photographed.

It started in February of 1901 when a fisherman named Al Dixon was setting his lines at the 100-fathom curve of Newport Beach, California. Dixon first became aware that something unusual was happening when he heard "the goddamdest loudest whistle that was ever made" from behind his back, over the bow of his boat. He dropped the line he was holding and spun around. A huge animal "with a face somewhat like a bulldog" was slowly sinking back into the sea about fifty feet away from his skiff. In the back of the slowly submerging face was a body built "like a straight roller coaster," which was a least two hundred feet long.

Dixon, open-mouthed, watched it disappear beneath the water and then, as he stared, a much smaller version of the same animal raised its head out of the water and portions of its body

166

also broke the surface of the calm sea. Two wicked canine teeth projected from the lower jaw. The smaller version of the monster moved slowly toward the skiff. Its mouth closed slightly and Dixon once again heard the peculiar high-pitched whistle, although somewhat softer than the first cry. As it drew almost abreast of the boat, it too sank below the surface of the water. A second later, one of Dixon's lines began to scream on its reel. Dixon didn't hesitate a second. He picked up the pole and reel and threw it as far from the skiff as he could. He then quickly cut his other lines and "started rowing like hell for shore." The larger monster surfaced, screamed toward him with its shrill whistle, "as if telling me to hurry up." Dixon needed no encouragement. He was exhausted by the time he reached the dock in Newport Bay.

"There's a big eel out there," he replied. "A couple of 'em. One's about two hundred feet long. The other's about twenty-five feet," he told a man on the pier. "They got away with all my gear."

His friend started to laugh, then stopped and turned his head away when he saw that Dixon was serious. By evening the story was all over town, and Al Dixon was being looked upon in about the same manner as the Norwegians had looked upon the good Bishop Pontoppidan.

About two weeks later, a young man named Joe Baracca decided to take a swim from the beach in an area that now has become the end of Thirty-sixth Street. Just beyond the surfing line, he noticed a fish pole lying in the water. Taking hold of it, he started back to shore. When he reached knee-deep water, he noticed for the first time that the other end of the fishing line was snagged on something in the water. He pulled on it tentatively, felt something give, then started to reel it in. A moment later, a huge body rose in the curl of a wave and raced toward him. Baracca dropped the pole and ran.

167

When the wave receded, the monster was lying on the sand. For a long while, Baracca watched it cautiously from a distance, then, satisfied that it was dead, he went back to it. Never had he seen anything like it. Two large canine teeth protruded from the lower jaw and there were smaller teeth in both the upper and lower jaws, with small spaces between. Through one of these ran the fishing line which continued on into the animal's stomach. The body was thick near the head, then gradually tapered down into a reptilian tail. Baracca pulled it farther up on the beach, then ran into the town to report its discovery.

Within the hour, half the town was out on the beach to look at the strange serpent with the head of a dog. The tailor in the town had his tape measure with him. The creature was thirty-one feet, six inches long. While he was measuring it, Al Dixon appeared, looked at it for a moment, then, taking a jackknife from his pocket, he cut the line and departed with his fishing pole. Several other men hauled the serpent further up on the beach. A photographer from Los Angeles, who was visiting Newport Beach, took a picture of the sea serpent with twenty-six of the town's residents posed behind it.

The local correspondent for the Los Angeles *Times* dutifully reported the discovery, but the editors apparently thought the tale of the find too unlikely to warrant printing it. The photographer, George Peabody, gave the photograph to the local Newport-Balboa *Press*, but this newspaper apparently also was short of space and did not bother using it.

Several years later, the photograph was given to Harry Welch, secretary of the Newport Beach Chamber of Commerce, who had copies made and sent one to the Los Angeles County Museum. A probable identification, that of an oarfish, was made by the museum; a fish that sometimes does grow to the length of thirty feet. Dixon knew better, however. "That one was the baby. The other was at least two hundred feet long."

168

No one can remember what happened to the baby sea serpent that swallowed Dixon's bait. It probably started to smell and was buried.

There is no mystery, however, as to what happened to one of the gigantic sixty-pound minnows that was caught in Lake Mojave, California. The first of these big minnows was caught by an Indian in November of 1952 and was rather well devoured by the fisherman and several of his friends before it came to the attention of the United States Fish and Wildlife Service. By the time a ranger reached the village, some cats had pretty well worked over the head of the strange fish, but there was enough left for the ranger to determine that the fish was of a species thought to have become extinct hundreds of thousands of years ago.

In November of 1962, a sports fisherman from Las Vegas, Nevada, caught another prehistoric sixty-two-pound minnow while fishing in Lake Mojave. This fisherman had never seen anything like it before and he took it to the Fish and Wildlife station for identification.

The Fish and Wildlife Department was ecstatic. It was in perfect condition. "You have caught a most rare, prehistoric fish," a ranger told the Las Vegan.

"No kidding," the fisherman replied.

"We'll preserve it and send it on to Washington," the ranger said excitedly.

The fisherman shook his head. "Like hell you will," he replied. "That's going over the mantel of my den."

The ranger shook his head and refused to give it back. While the ichthyologists gently prepared it for its long trip back to Washington, the Las Vegas sports fisherman went to court and demanded that his fish be returned to him. The judge thought his argument was a reasonable one. If a man who is properly licensed catches a fish, he is entitled to keep the fish.

169

The government fought back. The sixty-two-pound minnow lay in a carefully prepared preservative solution while the case was appealed and appealed once again. The government lost.

The giant prehistoric minnow now is mounted and hangs over a fireplace in a Las Vegas den.

A few miles to the southeast of Newport Beach, over the mountains and into the desert country, there is the legend of the abominable sandman. In January of 1964, a Marine major was exploring some of the more remote canyons in the lower Borrego Valley when he came across some incongruous tracks. Excitedly, he recalled the abominable snowman legend. The tracks were splay-toed and immense, staggered in some areas, parallel in others, with clearly definable digits which terminated in tiny depressions, as if made by claws. The prints pointed downhill, each pair falling at an interval of approximately forty inches from the preceding set. Upon reaching the desert floor, the tracks continued into the bed of a wash, then disappeared in the wind-blown sand of an arroyo. The major continued his search and found identical prints on a nearby hill, where there was some scrub grass and softer ground. These tracks were about seven feet apart and slightly larger than the others. From this, the major deduced that the monster which had made them was capable of prodigious leaps.

Upon his return to San Diego, the major went through the files of the San Diego *Union* and, although he found little on an abominable sandman, he did learn that some years earlier a monster had been killed by a Frank Cox at Deadman's Hole near Warner Hot Springs. This monster was described as having feet twenty-four inches long, weighing about four hundred pounds and with a small head and buck teeth. It appeared to be a cross between a man and a bear.

The following weekend, the major returned to the Borrego Valley and made several plaster casts of the tracks he had discovered. He then took pictures of the casts and wrote a story about his discovery, which he sold to *Desert Magazine*. Within a few days after the story was published, the Borrego Valley was swarming with explorers seeking the abominable sandman, a foray which caused considerable frustration to rangers in the Anza-Borrego State Park, who for months worked around the clock pulling the vehicles of abominable sandman hunters out of the deep sand.

One of the editors of *Desert Magazine* went to Borrego for a personal inspection of the phenomenon. She noticed a steer grazing on a scrub a short distance away. A few moments later, she noticed some dried dung lying on the ground. She kicked it aside and took a plaster cast of the impression left by the dung in the sand. The cast was virtually identical to the casts made by the curious major.

Not so easily explained is the mysterious Big Foot of the Pacific Northwest, sometimes known as the Sasquatch, which has been sighted in wilderness areas on many occasions, has been tracked for miles, and photographed by both motion picture and still camera.

According to many tribes of Indians, the Sasquatch has been around for centuries. The first known chronicled sighting of the eight-foot Big Foot appeared in the *Daily British Colonist* of Victoria, B.C., on June 30, 1884. The newspaper reported that the crew of a freight train which ran between Yale and Lytton in British Columbia had captured, alive, a Big Foot which had been sleeping near the railroad tracks. The monster was described as "half man and half beast" and was shaped like a human being. Except for its hands and feet, the body was covered with shiny black hair approximately an inch long. The creature was reported as being "extraordinarily strong, with forearms much longer than a man's. It had the ability to break a three-inch-thick stick by merely twisting it in its hands." The animal was in the possession

171

of a George Tibury of Yale. There appears to be no further record as to what Tibury did with his monstrous pet. About two weeks after the monster was captured, the train running between Lytton and Yale was wrecked and the more avid of the Big Foot fans contend that the wrecking of the train was an act of vengeance carried out by Big Foots because of the earlier capture.

Other sightings of Sasquatch have been compiled by writer James B. Shuman for the Los Angeles *Times*. Mike King, a timber cruiser, spotted one at a waterhole on Vancouver Island. Charles Flood of New Westminster saw another eating berries in 1915.

In 1924, a Big Foot scared the daylights out of some prospectors in two widely separated parts of the Pacific Northwest. The first incident occurred in July of that year at an isolated canyon near Mount St. Helens in Washington when a band of the giant Big Foots attacked a cabin where five prospectors were sleeping. Earlier in the day, one of the prospectors had shot at what he thought was a large bear. He thought he had killed it, but he could find no sign of the animal when he went into the trees to skin it. The Big Foots who assaulted the cabin threw huge boulders onto the roof and charged the door consistently, in an attempt to get past the barricade. They were driven off only after a number had been wounded by the guns of the prospectors.

The following morning, the prospectors went for help and a posse of deputy sheriffs, citizens, and reporters returned with them to the cabin. The building was badly damaged and, surrounding the cabin, were hundreds of giant footprints. The posse made a thorough search of the area, but the Big Foots had vanished.

A little more than a month later, a seventy-five-year-old prospector named Al Ostman drifted into Vancouver with an incredible story. He had been sleeping in his bag a couple of weeks earlier in a remote area about one hundred miles north of the city when he awoke to find himself being picked up off of the ground. He was slung "like a sack of flour" over the shoulder of a huge gorilla, who set off at a trot across country. Shortly after the break of dawn, he was dropped on the ground and knocked out. When he regained consciousness, he found that he had been removed from his sleeping bag and that he was surrounded by a family of Sasquatch. The females were around seven feet tall and the males at least a foot taller. Ostman said he was held captive by the Big Foots for six days, confined in a small bowl-shaped valley which had only one narrow exit. He escaped, he said, when he fed the Big Foot guarding the exit a tin of snuff, fleeing when the Big Foot rolled on the ground in a paroxysm of sneezing. Understandably, the adventure of Mr. Al Ostman attracted little attention.

According to Shuman, the next sighting that can be taken seriously occurred in September, 1941, when a Big Foot strolled into the isolated home of Mrs. George Chapman at Ruby Creek about thirty miles up the Fraser River from Agassiz, British Columbia. She and her three children fled out of the back door.

When she returned with her husband, the Big Foot had departed, taking along some salted fish. Donald Hunter, of the University of Oregon, saw a Big Foot in the Oregon Cascades near Todd Lake in 1942. His wife was a witness to the sighting of a Sasquatch, this one about nine feet tall. In 1955, William Roe of Edmonton, Canada, spotted another Big Foot on Mica Mountain, near the Indian village of Tête Jaune Cache in British Columbia.

In the summer of 1964, Scott Claghorn, an Arlington, Washington, newspaper publisher, went for a Sunday afternoon drive with his wife. Early in the evening, well before dusk, they were heading back toward Arlington on a little-used road about thirty miles east of the community, when he noticed two giants running across an open field. They were so tall that Claghorn instinctively jammed on his brakes for a better look. The squealing of the tires apparently caught their attention, as the two "giants" stopped, straightened up, and stared toward the car.

"Two Big Foots," Claghorn said in amazement. Slowly, he reached for his camera lying on the back seat of the car. The Sasquatch apparently noticed the movement, for suddenly they ran at an incredible speed toward a clump of trees, where they disappeared.

"I always thought they were a myth," Claghorn said a few moments later. "It's a hell of a story."

"You've been on the wagon for twenty years," his wife said. "Everyone will think you have fallen off."

"I won't say they were Big Foots. I'll just say they were two ten-foot giants wearing fur fatigue suits."

"Not even that," his wife said firmly. "It will ruin our circulation."

Claghorn sadly agreed. Only a few close friends know of his experience.

Roger Patterson, a thirty-five-year-old rancher from Yakima, Washington, was luckier with his camera. His avocation has been running down the legend of the Big Foot. He probably has the most complete collection of sightings in existence and he is the author of a book entitled *Do Abominable Snowmen of America Really Exist?* which is a rhetorical title, as he is convinced that they do. He even has a sixteen-millimeter motion picture film of a Sasquatch in action to prove it.

The film was shot in October of 1967. Shortly before it was taken, a Big Foot-phile telephoned Patterson to report that Big Foot tracks of recent origin had been found near Bluff Creek in northern California. Patterson, accompanied by an expert tracker named Robert Gimlin, departed immediately for California where, for the next week and a half they scouted the area searching for some signs of the elusive hominid. On the afternoon

174

of October 20, as they rounded a bend in a canyon, Patterson's horse suddenly reared and, as the rancher brought the animal under control, he saw the Big Foot.

"He was about one hundred and twenty-five feet across a creek," he says. "Its head was human, although more slanted and with a large forehead and wide, broad nostrils. Its arms hung almost to its knees when it walked. Its hair was two to four inches long, brown underneath, lighter at the top and covering the entire body, except for the face around the nose, mouth and cheek. And it was a female. It had big, pendulous breasts."

This Big Foot was more cooperative than the ones seen by the Claghorns. It moved slowly across a sandbar, but Patterson had time to get out his motion picture camera and start shooting. He had time to use up a full roll before the Sasquatch ambled into some nearby woods and disappeared.

The rancher next made plaster casts of some of the footprints and covered the others with bark, in order that they could be studied by experts. One of the experts was Robert Titmus, of Kitimat, British Columbia, who measured the tracks. After a close study, he pronounced that they were undoubtedly not a hoax and were made by a creature he had never seen. Each track was fourteen and one half inches long and from the deepness of the impression, Titmus estimated they were made by an animal weighing between six and seven hundred pounds.

There were some who branded the film a hoax. Others, equally expert, claimed it was not. The great Pacific Northwest is still a wilderness area of more than 150,000 square miles, so it is entirely possible that there could be an unknown species of animal living somewhere within its confines.

The Norwegians did not believe the story of Bishop Pontoppidan and his sea serpent, yet a fisherman named Al Dixon caught one off Newport Beach. Few people believed that gigantic

175

prehistoric minnows still cavorted in Lake Mojave until two of them were caught.

Someday, someone may catch a Sasquatch, if he is man enough.

A LOST SHIP OF THE DESERT

There are many who swear that camels still roam the deserts of the United States Southwest. Prospectors often come back into town with a story that while they were sitting alone near some saguaro cactus, or some greasewood, or some cholla, they saw anywhere from one to fifty camels silently moving past, silhouetted in the light of a full moon. One of these tales was proved beyond all doubt when, shortly after it was reported, some drivers recaptured a trio of camels who had escaped the annual Date Festival celebration in Indio, California. A number of years ago, however, there were many camels roaming the American deserts. They were brought to this country by the United States Army and large numbers of them were turned loose when the experiment in camels was brought to an end.

Most credit the idea of importing camels to Edward F. Beale, who was undoubtedly the greatest military publicity hound of the mid-nineteenth century. The idea for the drafting of camels into the United States Army first was suggested by a Major George H. Crossman, who thought they would do well as beasts of burden in Florida. Crossman's idea was pigeonholed until 1848, when Major Henry C. Wayne suggested to the War Department that a camel purchasing expedition be sent to the Middle East and that the ungainly beasts be used for transporting military supplies in the American Southwest. When the War Department failed to act, Wayne took his idea to Jefferson Davis, who was a senator at the time.

In 1853, after President Franklin Pierce had appointed Davis as Secretary of War, Davis once again resurrected the plan. If the camel was a "ship of the desert" in the Sahara and the Sind, Davis reasoned, then there was no reason why he could not fulfill the same function in the Mojave and Death Valley. Accordingly, the United States Camel Corps was established and Wayne, accompanied by Navy Lieutenant David Porter, set sail for the Middle East two years later on board the Navy ship *Supply*. Their assignment was to buy camels.

Their first port of call was Tunis, North Africa, where they soon found that dealers in the used-camel market were about as ethical as a Los Angeles used-car dealer today. They discovered, also, that there were many different kinds of camels. There was a dromedary who came with one hump and a Bactrian who came with two. Some camels were slow and could carry heavy loads. Others were fast, but with a much lighter capacity for carrying weight.

Wayne spent a few hundred dollars of the War Department's funds on some camels here, loaded them on the *Supply*, and continued on to Smyrna, Turkey, which, he had been told, was the Detroit of the camel market.

Before the *Supply* cleared the harbor, one of his camels died and was given a quick burial at sea. Another developed a camel's itch, which Wayne soon learned was an itch to end all itches. While Wayne was being treated for this ailment, the beast from which he had caught it broke loose, jumped into the Mediterranean and started swimming back toward North Africa. There apparently is no record as to whether or not the camel made it.

When the Navy ship put in at Smyrna, customs officials came aboard. Five of the camels on board the *Supply* would have to be kept on board in their pens. A camel's hump that sagged over onto its side did not mean that the camel was young and approaching adult life, the officials explained to Wayne. It meant that the beast was either very old or very sick and camels this sick were not going to be allowed in Turkey.

The *Supply* put out to sea, where mass services were held for the dying camels before they also were pitched over the side. By the time the *Supply* returned to Smyrna, Wayne had decided that he needed a professional consultant. After a considerable search, he found one man who appeared to be reasonably honest, was an expert on camels, and was willing to join the United States Camel Corps as a paid consultant and to recruit other camel drivers, who would return to the United States and train enlisted men in the art of camel driving. This man was Hadji Ali, which was pronounced Hi Jolly forevermore by all the Americans with whom he came in contact.

Hi Jolly took over the War Department's mission. He saw that proper camel pens were built on board the *Supply* and he bought 28 camels. The price was high, but the beasts all appeared reasonably healthy. Hi Jolly also rounded up a half-dozen other

179

camel drivers who had no objections to coming to the United States.

Four of the camels died en route to the New World, but six baby camels were born on shipboard, so when the *Supply* docked at Indianola, Texas, on May 14, 1856, there was a total of thirty camels on board. There was a large crowd present to watch the unloading.

The camels were very docile while they were led down the gangplank, but as soon as they hit solid earth, their attitude changed. "They reared and kicked and cried, broke their halters, tore up picket lines and pawed and bit each other. The Indianola mothers who had come to the docks to see the strange beasts, gathered up their children and fled."

"Those are just the pehlevans, or wrestling camels," Hi Jolly explained. "They are very fast and good for chasing Indians."

"What about those who are spitting on everyone?" Wayne asked.

Hi Jolly shrugged. "Maybe it's because they have never seen anyone wearing such funny clothes," he said.

Among those on hand to greet the camels was the ubiquitous Edward Beale with orders in his possession to take charge of the camels and relieve Wayne.

Beale first led the camel caravan to Camp Verde, Texas, some sixty miles northwest of San Antonio, and it was on this trek the United States Army first learned that the Americanization of the camel was not going to be as easy as it had appeared on paper. Whenever Hi Jolly or one of the six other camel drivers brought from the mid-East spoke to one of the "ships of the desert," the beast would respond immediately. The only language the camels seemed to understand was Arabic. Not one camel in the lot would learn English and not one American soldier in the caravan would learn Arabic. Beale tried to overcome this language barrier while the camels were penned in Camp Verde, but to no avail.

Beale accused Hi Jolly of not cooperating sufficiently. Hi Jolly protested vehemently. The next day he went to see Beale once again. The gist of the conversation was that all of the Arabs were homesick, an illness that possibly could be cured quickly if their salaries were doubled. Beale followed Hi Jolly's advice. For more than a year, the camels were kept at Camp Verde. During this time, an additional forty-one were brought across the Atlantic. The second shipment was made under the tutelage of a good friend of Hi Jolly's, a George Xaralampo who, forevermore, was to be known as George the Greek.

On June 25, 1857, the United States Camel Corps, under Beale's command and Hi Jolly's authority, departed Texas for an overland trek across the deserts to Camp Drumm, which is now within the city of Los Angeles. According to Beale, the trip was an outstanding success. Beale explained it in a long letter to Jefferson Davis. "When there is plenty of water, the mule has no desire to drink. There is no way to explain to the mule that for the next ten days water is going to be scarce. When there is no water, the mule wants a drink. The camels, on the contrary, drink gallons of water at one time and never suffer from thirst, no matter what the nature of the country, for another ten days or more."

It was an interesting observation, coming, as it did, more than a year and a half after the camels had been purchased.

The cross-country trip took five months. Shortly after arriving at Camp Drumm, Beale moved on to better things. The camels chewed their cuds when they were not breeding, which was rarely. By the end of 1859, the camel count was in excess of two hundred. The soldiers of the Camel Corps had little to do. George the Greek bought a ranch in El Monte.

When the Civil War broke out a short time later, the Camel Corps was brought to the attention of the new Secretary of War, Edwin M. Stanton, and he immediately ordered the government to sever all connections with the project that had been the idea of his Confederate predecessor. Several of the camels were driven over the mountains to the desert and turned loose.

The officers in charge at Camp Drumm then decided that this might not be a practical manner for getting rid of them. They met regularly to debate an alternative method which could evoke no criticism from Washington.

In 1864, Stanton found out that the Army still had a camel corps in California. Angrily, he ordered that all of the camels be driven from Camp Drumm to Benecia, California, many hundreds of miles to the north, and sold at public auction. George the Greek was too busy at his ranch to make the trip. When Hi Jolly insisted that he could not move all of them north by himself, George the Greek compromised. He took half of the herd, drove it over the desert, and turned it loose. As nearly as can be determined, about four hundred camels were given their freedom in this manner.

Hi Jolly took about one hundred up to the Benecia Arsenal north of San Francisco, where they were put up for public auction on February 28, 1864. There was only one bidder, a Samuel McCleneghan, who had an idea that he could use them for transportation between Sacramento and the silver boom town of Austin, Nevada.

Hi Jolly and the five camel drivers from the mid-East agreed to work for McCleneghan. When the caravan reached Sacramento, however, Hi Jolly and his friends suddenly were seized by another attack of homesickness. McCleneghan explained that he did not have the unlimited resources of the United States War Department and a compromise was reached. McCleneghan and Hi Jolly would put on a camel race at the annual state fair, which was just opening in Sacramento.

The race was well-publicized and more than two-thousand

Californians paid a dollar admission to witness the Great Dromedary Race "brought directly to this fair from Smyrna, Turkey."
Whether or not McClenaghan made any money on the betting
that accompanied the race is unknown. Hi Jolly cleared two
thousand dollars in gate receipts.

When the fair ended, the remnants of the United States
Camel Corps were moved to Austin. The welcome McClenaghan
and Hi Jolly received there was less than welcome. It started
when a horse shied as the caravan entered the town, which in turn
caused one of the camels to break loose. Before the incident had
ended, every "horse and mule within the town limits had disappeared."

A contract was arranged, however, with the owner of an
ore reduction plant to haul in supplies and other material from both
Virginia City and Carson City, but it did not last long. Oddly,
although the camels had traversed from Texas to California without causing any trouble, they were a source of constant friction
to the native Nevadans. Horses and mules inevitably panicked
every time a camel caravan entered a town. Virginia City passed
an ordinance prohibiting the use of camels within the town limits.
A short time later, the Nevada legislature passed a law outlawing
the use of camels on a public thoroughfare, thus making that
usually tolerant state the only state in the union that has an anti-
camel ordinance on its books.

The day the law became effective, Hi Jolly once again
became sick. This time it was not a longing for his native Turkey
that troubled him. It was a more serious disease: gold fever, an
ailment for which there is no cure. Hi Jolly did one more favor
for McClenaghan before he took off. He drove the camel herd a
few miles outside of Austin and turned every one of them loose
on the desert. The next morning, Hi Jolly left for Arizona on a
mule with a burro in tow and a complete prospecting outfit. Mc-
Clenaghan went back to San Francisco. Hi Jolly eventually

married a Gertrude Serna in Tucson. He died in the small town of Quartzite, Arizona, in 1902. His gravestone is a pyramid with a camel effigy at its apex.

Most of the camels that were turned loose in Nevada moved south to the warmer deserts of California and Arizona. Many were killed by Apaches, who discovered camel meat was a tasty dish. In 1913, a herd of camels was pursued by a posse near Ajo, but easily outdistanced the horses in the soft sand. There are many who still claim to sight camels in the more remote sections of the Southwest, but, unlike the Big Foot, no one ever has come close enough to take pictures of them.

One of the camels that roams the area is a ghostly beast known as the Flying Dutchman of the Desert. According to the legend, one of the officers of the Camel Corps decided upon a unique punishment for an unruly enlisted man. One evening, as the original caravan was making camp near the Gila River, the officer decided that he would force the soldier to learn to ride a camel. He chose the biggest beast in the herd, a Bactrian, and had the soldier's legs tied to the saddle of the animal.

When the camel rocked to its feet, it suddenly broke away and raced off in the general direction of Death Valley. (The soldier quickly died in the intense heat.) Despite a three-day search, no trace of the soldier or the camel could be found. Soon the soldier's body became a skeleton that fell apart, all except for for the legs that still were tied to the huge camel, which roams Death Valley to this day.

The Flying Dutchman of the Desert is easily recognized by the slash of white on his saddle, the skeletal legs of the unruly soldier in the United States Camel Corps.

EPILOGUE

THE LOST GOLD BARS OF JUAN BLANCO

In the mid-sixties, a new tale of buried gold began to circulate among the fraternity of treasure seekers in the Southwest. The details were vague. The only information that was consistent was that a part of a large hoard of Dominican gold bars had been found somewhere near Tecate, Mexico, a small border town a few miles east of Tijuana. Soon it became a legend.

The source of the story was discovered in late 1966 by a young engineer from Los Angeles named Paul Devlin.

After spending a weekend in Enseñada, Devlin started out on his return drive to Los Angeles. As he neared Tijuana, the traffic became heavier and he remembered the early Sunday eve-

185

ning jam at the border as thousands of United States citizens returned home from the bullfights, the races at Agua Caliente, and shopping sprees into Tijuana. About the time this thought occurred to him, he noticed a square pink building on top of a small hill some distance from the highway. A narrow, rutted road led up to it and at the junction was a Coca-Cola and a Dos Equis beer sign with an arrow pointing toward the building. It was the beer sign that sent Devlin up the rough road.

Originally, the building had been constructed as a private home. A partition between two small rooms had been knocked out to make room for a very small bar and restaurant. There was only one patron, a man who appeared to be in his late sixties with snow-white hair and nut-brown skin drawn tightly over the high cheekbones of his face. When Devlin sat down, the old man looked at him incuriously for a moment, then turned away and stared at the bottle of tequila in front of him. Near his right hand was a dish with quartered limes, a shot glass, and a salt cellar.

"Good evening," Devlin said politely, but the man did not answer. His voice, however, caused a reaction in the room in back of the bar, for he heard a chair being pushed back. Presently an enormously fat woman appeared. She looked at him in surprise, then after he placed his order, giggled delightedly and opened a bottle of Dos Equis for him.

"Not many tourists come here," the woman said, with another giggle.

"I do not think of myself as a tourist, señora," he replied in Spanish. "I think of myself as a guest in your country."

The old man turned on his chair, stared at Devlin for a moment, then with a steady hand, poured the shot glass full of tequila. "You speak our language well, señor," he said.

"You are very kind, señor."

The old man wiped his mouth with the back of his hand, then turned toward Devlin. His eyes were a deep black that contrasted sharply with his thick, white eyebrows. "I do not like gringos," he said.

"That is a pity," Devlin replied.

"Calm yourself, Don Juan," the fat woman said.

"You calm yourself," the old man retorted. "The gentleman is not a gringo. He is a *Norteamericano*." He stood up and held out his hand. "Allow me the honor of presenting myself. I am called Juan Blanco."

Devlin stood up, shook the proffered hand and introduced himself, then slid back on his stool.

"I will tell you why I do not like gringos," Señor Blanco said presently. He poured another shot of tequila in his glass. "Would you like to hear why I myself do not like the gringos?"

"Why not?"

The fat woman sighed and went back to the other room.

Devlin sipped his beer and listened to the old man recount his tale of woe. Two days after Easter, in 1960, two men had arrived at his farm in Tecate. They arrived in a brand-new Lincoln and they wore very expensive suits that seemed to change color as they moved in the sunlight. One of the men tried to speak in Spanish, but he spoke the language so badly that Juan Blanco was forced to send for his young grandson to act as an interpreter. The two men wanted to buy his farm, they told Juan Blanco, and the price they offered for the land was more than twice its value. They were very disappointed when Juan Blanco explained the law. No foreigner could buy land in Mexico within thirty miles of a border. Then the two men withdrew a short distance and talked to each other in English, apparently forgetting that Juan Blanco's grandson, who was squatting on the ground, could understand them and was translating their conversation to his grandfather.

It developed that the two men had discovered a bar of gold buried in the ground in the United States just across the border from Tecate and they also had found a map buried in a tube of lead which told of the location of many similar bars of gold, a treasure hidden by the Dominicans after their missions had been abandoned. The larger of the two gringos became angry with his companion. He said repeatedly it would be easy to come back during the night and dig it up and that the old farmer, who was Juan Blanco, never would know. The smaller man would not agree to this. He argued that they should tell the old farmer of the discovery and, because the treasure was on his land, it was right that he should have half of it, and that also there was so much gold that even after it was divided, they all would be rich.

Eventually the bigger man threw up his hands and agreed to the plan of his friend. When they came back and told Juan Blanco of the treasure, he acted surprised and happy. They showed him the map found in the lead tube. The words upon it were written in a strange language which the smaller gringo identified as Latin, a language he knew well, he said, because he had studied for the priesthood as a boy.

The two gringos carried a metal detecting machine in the trunk of their expensive car and the smaller man showed Juan Blanco how it worked and let him operate it. The map was very accurate. Juan Blanco himself, with the aid of the machine, found the location of the treasure in little more than an hour. The cache was in an area just out of sight of the highway. Juan Blanco himself dug up the first bar, which was next to another tube of lead. The bar was very heavy. On one side was an etched cross and on the other, the word *ora*. The smaller gringo, the one who was honest, picked up the lead tube, scraped away the wax around one end with his penknife, then extracted a very old piece of parchment paper. He unrolled it carefully and after he had finished reading it, he crossed himself.

He showed the old paper to the big gringo and Juan Blanco. This, too, was written in Latin, he said, and it told that directly below them were buried two thousand golden bars identical to the one they had discovered. They could not, however, dig it up immediately. The smaller gringo read the contents of the old paper. If the gold, he translated, had not been recovered by a Dominican priest before it was found by another person, then this was God's will. If it were found by another, there were certain requirements that must be met before it was removed from the ground. The finder must journey to the City of Mexico and pay for 365 masses at the basilica. If, when he returned, the gold was still in its burial ground, then it was God's will that it become the property of the finder. The finder could pay for his trip and the masses with the golden bar that had been left by the tube. If these instructions were not followed, then the finder would be confined to hell forever.

The big gringo laughed, then picked up the shovel and started to dig. His friend became very angry and pulled the shovel away. If these instructions were not followed, he cried, they all three would be confined to hell for eternity. The big man sighed and became quiet.

Juan Blanco covered up the hole and they walked back to the house. The big gringo took some scales from his car, weighed the gold bar, then whistled. Its weight was worth two thousand American dollars, he said. They were millionaires, for there were two thousand more identical bars in the ground.

There was the question of the conditions, the smaller man reminded them. The answer was simple, the other gringo said. The old man, Juan Blanco, should go to Mexico City because he was the one who actually had found the treasure. Juan Blanco shook his head. He was needed on the farm, he told them through his grandson, but the real reason he would not go was because the big gringo was a thief who would return when no one was at the farm and steal all of the treasure. For a long time they discussed the problem and it became evident that the smaller gringo did not trust his companion, either.

The small gringo offered another solution. His friend

189

would make the trip to Mexico City by airplane from Tijuana
and he would pay for the masses. He could easily be back within
three days and then they could all recover the gold together.

His companion at first objected because he did not know
how to ask a padre to say a mass. The big gringo thought for a
moment, then said both of them would go to Mexico City and
that Juan Blanco would do something to show his good faith, such
as letting them hold five thousand United States dollars of his
while they were gone. Again, the smaller man, the one who had
studied for the priesthood, objected.

Juan Blanco became tired of the bickering. He offered an
alternative. He would give them two thousand dollars and they
would leave behind the gold bar that had been discovered next to
the tube. The two gringos agreed to it, apparently not realizing
that Juan Blanco had outwitted them because the bar they had
discovered was worth the two thousand dollars. That very afternoon, they drove to the bank in Tijuana where Juan Blanco withdrew two thousand dollars, which was almost all of the money he
had in the bank. He gave it to the smaller man, who was more
honest, and the smaller man gave him a receipt for it as they drove
back to Tecate in the shiny new Lincoln.

For a week, Juan Blanco remained on his farm checking
constantly to see that no one disturbed the ground where the
treasure was buried. On the eighth day, he became suspicious. He
took his gold bar to Tijuana where an examination disclosed it to
be a piece of bronze-plated lead.

Devlin rapped the bottom of his beer bottle on the counter
and the fat woman came in and took another from the cooler.
"Did you tell the police, Señor Blanco?"

"Of course. They laughed." He reached into his pocket
and pulled out his wallet from which he extracted a small piece of
ruled paper. He passed it to Devlin. It was a receipt for two
thousand United States dollars signed by John Doe, at what un-

doubtedly was a fictitious address in Los Angeles. "You know why they laughed so hard, Señor Devlin?"

"Possibly because the name John Doe in English is used for someone whose real name is unknown."

The old man nodded. "This is partly the reason, my friend." He poured tequila into the shot glass. "Do you know the name that is used on such occasions in Mexico?"

Devlin shook his head.

"It is Juan Blanco . . . my very own name." The old man laughed, upended the shot glass and bit into the fresh lime. Then he pushed himself to his feet. "For the night, I think I shall take one of your rooms, Gordita," he said.

"At your orders, Don Juan."

Juan Blanco nodded toward the woman, then bowed gravely toward Devlin before he walked steadily out of the door.

"He should have taken his shotgun and told them to go back to the United States in their shiny new Lincoln." Devlin signaled Gordita to join him in a beer.

"Then he would have not learned about the gold on his farm," she answered.

Devlin laughed. "But there was no gold."

"At the time, he did not know this," she gestured with the beer bottle. "What if there had been many bars of gold? Surely he should find out first if the gold was there."

"That is the whole point. He did not find out. He should have dug the hole deeper."

"How could he do that? If the gold was there, then he would have been disobeying the orders of the padres and would be sent to hell for all eternity."

Devlin smiled. "You are a logical woman, Gordita," he replied. "It was a problem."

"No, señor, it was not a problem. It was a matter of faith."

Some three months later, Devlin was at a small party in

191

Los Angeles where someone told the story of a vast Dominican treasure that had been buried in Tecate. In turn, Devlin repeated the experience of Juan Blanco. The man who had told the story agreed that such a thing could have happened, but, he added, this did not necessarily mean that a Dominican treasure was not buried in Tecate.

Legends start from fact. They are kept alive through faith.